On Ethics, Politics and Psychology in the Twenty-First Century

READING AUGUSTINE

Series Editor:

Miles Hollingworth

Reading Augustine offers personal and close readings of St Augustine of Hippo from leading philosophers and religious scholars. Its aim is to make clear Augustine's importance to contemporary thought and to present Augustine not only or primarily as a pre-eminent Christian thinker but as a philosophical, spiritual, literary and intellectual icon of the West.

Volumes in the series:

On Ethics, Politics and Psychology in the Twenty-First Century
John Rist

On Love, Confession, Surrender and the Moral Self
Ian Clausen

On Education, Formation, Citizenship and the Lost Purpose of Learning
Joseph Clair

On Creativity, Liberty, Love and the Beauty of the Law
Todd Breyfogle

On Consumer Culture, Identity, the Church and the Rhetorics of Delight (forthcoming)
Mark Clavier

On Self-Harm, Narcissism, Atonement and the Vulnerable Christ (forthcoming)
David Vincent Meconi

On God, The Soul, Evil and the Rise of Christianity (forthcoming)
John Peter Kenney

On Music, Sound, Affect and Ineffability (forthcoming)
Carol Harrison

On Ethics, Politics and Psychology in the Twenty-First Century

John Rist

With an interview with Bishop Austin Redivivus orchestrated by Anna Rist

Bloomsbury Academic
An imprint of Bloomsbury Publishing Inc

BLOOMSBURY
NEW YORK • LONDON • OXFORD • NEW DELHI • SYDNEY

Bloomsbury Academic

An imprint of Bloomsbury Publishing Inc

1385 Broadway	50 Bedford Square
New York	London
NY 10018	WC1B 3DP
USA	UK

www.bloomsbury.com

BLOOMSBURY and the Diana logo are trademarks of Bloomsbury Publishing Plc

First published 2018

Library of Congress Cataloging-in-Publication Data
Names: Rist, John M., author.
Title: On ethics, politics and psychology in the twenty-first century /
John Rist ; with an interview with Bishop Austin
Redivivus orchestrated by Anna Rist.
Description: New York : Bloomsbury Academic, 2017. |
Series: Reading Augustine | Includes index.
Identifiers: LCCN 2017015998 (print) | LCCN 2017029471 (ebook) |
ISBN 9781501307508 (ePub) | ISBN 9781501307515 (ePDF) |
ISBN 9781501307492 (hardcover : alk. paper)
Subjects: LCSH: Augustine, Saint, Bishop of Hippo. | Ethics.
Classification: LCC B655.Z7 (ebook) | LCC B655.Z7 R483 2017 (print) |
DDC 170–dc23
LC record available at https://lccn.loc.gov/2017015998

ISBN:	HB:	978-1-5013-0749-2
	PB:	978-1-5013-0748-5
	ePub:	978-1-5013-0750-8
	ePDF:	978-1-5013-0751-5

Series: Reading Augustine

Cover design: Catherine Wood
Cover image © Urbancow / iStock

Typeset by Integra Software Services Pvt. Ltd.
Printed and bound in the United States of America

CONTENTS

ACKNOWLEDGEMENT

Various friends have made helpful suggestions for this book, most of which I have accepted. I would like particularly to thank Kevin White for his encouragement, and Robert Sokolowski for reading an earlier version of the entire manuscript and making some splendid comments, all of which I have tried to take into account. The assistance I have received from Anna Rist is, of course, especially apparent in the 'orchestrated' interview with Bishop Austin, but is far from limited to that. As usual, her sharp criticism has made the whole text clearer and more readable than I could have achieved on my own.

LIST OF ABBREVIATIONS

Most translations are my own. However, on certain occasions, I have quoted from R. W. Dyson's translation of *The City of God* (Cambridge University Press, 1998) and Edmund Hill's translation of *On the Trinity* (New City Press, 2012). These are clearly indicated in the text. For the interested reader, the most readily accessible English editions of Augustine's works are those in the series, *The Works of Saint Augustine, a Translation for the 21st Century* (New City Press, 1990–).

A2	Against Two Letters of the Pelagians
AJ	Against Julian of Eclanum
AS	Against the Sceptics
C	Confessions
CG	The City of God
E	Enchiridion
HR	On Human Responsibility
IW	Incomplete Work against Julian
JE	On John's Epistle
JG	On John's Gospel
L	Letters
PJ	On the Perfection of Justice
PRS	On the Predestination of the Saints
Ps	On Psalms

R	Reconsiderations
RS	Reply to Simplicianus
S	Sermons
T	On the Trinity
TR	On True Religion
UB	On the Usefulness of Belief

Introduction: What's a One-Time Bishop of Hippo Got to Do with the Third Millennium?

It may seem strange to resuscitate a pre-modern Christian thinker and turn him loose among the public intellectuals, the Kantians, rights-theorists, Hobbesians, consequentialists, liberals and celebs of our present Western society. And why fasten on Augustine, rather than on Anselm, Aquinas or other pre-Renaissance thinkers? That question, at least, is easily answered: since almost all intellectual debate in the contemporary West is carried on in narrowly conventional, secular and liberal terms – even when conducted by 'conservatives' or 'left-wingers' – it can be both refreshing and constructive to reintroduce the man whose extraordinary achievement it was to set the framework and tone of intellectual life from the fifth century to the eighteenth and beyond (even if less universally after the Reformation). Ideally, I would present him in dialogue – Platonic style – with some of our contemporary gurus and talking heads, but, though my wife has secured a radio interview with Augustine, the transcript of which appears at the end of this book, anything further would be a project beyond my capacity. My approach has therefore been more modest, and doubtless less effective; still, it allows 'Augustine' to speak in his own name. And perhaps this more modest approach retains something Platonic: just as Plato presents Socrates continuing to think 'socratically' after his death – the Platonic Socrates philosophizing as his original would have done had he lived longer – so 'our' Augustine, I believe, continues the work of his historical original.

A further reason why Augustine is more suited to reincarnation than any medieval thinker is that his world is much more like ours. In the medieval 'centuries of faith', though there were, of course, dissidents, on the whole there were agreed parameters within which philosophical and theological speculation occurred; intellectual life was comparatively homogenized. In Augustine's time, as in our own, the world was full of radically conflicting ideas, conflicting gods or idols, and consequently radically conflicted individuals. Everyone finds it easy to suppose that, as they have one head, so correspondingly they possess one set of more or less coherent beliefs; but especially in our world, as Alasdair MacIntyre and others have pointed out, such a view is manifestly false: we live in an intellectual stewpot in which bits of Christianity swirl around with bits of Marxism, Darwinism, Freudianism and countless others 'isms', almost guaranteeing that, unless we attend to our thoughts very carefully, we act in logically contradictory fashion for logically contradictory reasons. In such a world, Augustine believes, it is best first to examine unblinkingly what we are actually like. In the twenty-first century he might tell God it would be better he himself be brought back to life, rather than, say, Aquinas, for he described man as he is, his Dominican successor more as what he ought to be. But how – by what noble rhetoric – Augustine will ask, are we to move from what is to what ought to be? For him, that was, and it remains, the most important question of all.

Augustine has played a unique role in the development of Western culture. There were, of course, many great poets, philosophers and historians before him in ancient Greece and Rome, but the increasing dominance of Christianity, which added Hebrew wisdom to the inherited conglomerate, combined with the collapse of Roman authority and with it much of Greco-Roman civilization in Africa, Spain, Italy, France and England – it had never had much effect in most of Germany – led to a situation in which we can recognize Augustine as one of the last representatives of an educational system and culture soon to be largely forgotten or known only in near-mythological expositions. Yet though he was one of the last of the old school, he was also the most prominent of the new.

Augustine knew classical Latin literature well: many of its poets – Virgil, Ovid and Terence, its philosophers like Seneca, many of its

historians, especially Livy and Sallust, as well as the vastly erudite
Varro, and obviously its orators, especially Cicero. By contrast,
he had comparatively little first-hand knowledge of pre-Christian
texts in Greek, being for philosophical writing of that earlier age
largely dependent on what he could glean from the Latin, especially
from Cicero, Seneca and Varro. In his generation the Greek- and
Latin-speaking cultures within the Roman Empire were for various
reasons drifting ever further apart, but in addition to his familiarity
with Latin-speaking Christians such as Tertullian and Cyprian (not
to speak of the schismatic ex-Donatist exegete Tyconius), he came
to know much near-contemporary Greek philosophical thought,
albeit largely in translation: especially that of the Neoplatonists
Plotinus and Porphyry, as well as, in later life, something of the
writings of a few Greek-speaking Christian bishops.

In sharp contrast to Augustine's wide knowledge of at least Latin
culture, in the millennium after his death few in the West knew
much of the writers, whether pagan or Christian, of the Greco-
Roman society that had passed away – nor at first-hand of much
Greek-language *theology*. Whatever knowledge they had of the
pagan past and its long-gone philosophical distinction was acquired
chiefly from a limited selection of Augustine's own vast output,
eked out first by Boethius and later by translations of the sixth-
century Greek theologian known to us as Pseudo-Dionysius. Thus,
Augustine became the funnel through which his very personalized
version of the past reached the medievals, or a hinge to the door
that opened the future to antiquity.

Latin translations of Plotinus, a major influence on Augustine's
own thinking, were not available in the West for about a thousand
years after his death, Marsilio Ficino's first version appearing in 1494,
ten years after his Latin Plato. This strange historical circumstance
explains why, philosophically speaking, Western thought after 400
largely began again with Augustine, to be, as the centuries passed,
gradually enriched by the recovery of earlier figures: Aristotle (and
his Greek and Arabic commentators) in the thirteenth century,
Plato (often wildly misunderstood as Plotinus, or even Proclus) in
the fifteenth, while by 1600 various Stoic, Sceptic and Epicurean
writers had been recovered or at least better reconstructed.

But although Augustine was intellectually dominant, his works
were known only in part until the age of print, and his warnings
as to the necessity of reading them in chronological order were

neglected even after that. Although we cannot quite say that each medieval writer invented his own over-systematized Augustine, there is a certain truth in that claim, and only serious philological activity since the late eighteenth century has brought us to a situation in which we are able to evaluate in its original context the development of Augustine's thought from his conversion till his death over forty years later, in 430. Furthermore, despite a certain continuing sectarian resistance, we are increasingly able to untangle Augustine's concerns and solutions from the eisegesis of those who have wanted to appropriate him for their own theological purposes both in the Middle Ages and during and after the Reformation and Counter-Reformation. The long battle to restore the fifth-century Augustine is now almost – not quite yet – won.

Nevertheless, even the fact that such a battle has had to be fought is revealing, indicating as it does that what can now be reasonably presented as the ever-developing thought of Augustine is not always what Augustine has been taken to teach. That historical idiosyncrasy arises because, for hundreds of years after his death, everyone in the West purported to be an Augustinian – while thereafter almost everyone claimed in significant respects to be anti-Augustinian. Augustine's name was invoked not only on behalf of various disputed claims in the Middle Ages but also, as we have noted, in Reformation and Counter-Reformation disputes: thus Calvin was able to trumpet (*Institutes* 3.22.8) that 'Augustine is entirely with us'. All of which reveals that traditional discussion of 'Augustine' concerned itself as much with localized disputes in the thirteenth or sixteenth centuries as with the questions which in the fifth century Augustine was actually disputing.

Later writers were misled by mangled versions of the topics that concerned Augustine himself, so that many medieval and post-medieval thinkers, assuming themselves to be 'Augustinians' – at least from the eleventh century, the time of Anselm and Abelard – defended positions which certainly the mature Augustine – as probably also the earlier Augustine – would have repudiated. As I have already observed, Augustine was treated as a systematic thinker, and all such systematizing, even with persons far more systematic than Augustine, is liable to generate confusion; yet we have to recognize, however strange it may seem, that this approach was normal down to the end of the eighteenth century (and still in places persists).

Just *how* strange it is can be seen not only by wondering what sort of philosophical monster would be produced by treating Kant or Wittgenstein in the same way (thus generating philosophical claims to which those thinkers would at *no* time have wholly subscribed), but even by considering our own lives; how many of us would be happy to have to suppose that we had exactly the same ideas at the ages of twenty, thirty and seventy? Yet that is what systematizers, driven by mere conservatism, or worse by intellectual laziness, have in effect claimed for Augustine (among many others). Which is not to say that we cannot find a certain *continuity* – which is not *identity* – in the thought of serious intellectuals, indeed of most members of the human race. As Newman put it, 'Pass a number of years, and I find myself in another place. How? The whole man moves: paper logic is but the record of it' (*Apologia* [London 1908] 169). Yet it is the same 'I', or so I would insist. Were it not, the history would be of no interest.

That being the situation puts us in a position to recognize the main features of Augustine's thought: how that thought developed, and why, and so to get some idea of what he would do – without betraying his own insights, yet aware of the philosophical, scientific and general cultural activity that has taken place between his time and ours – if he could be reincarnated in the twenty-first-century West and asked to confront our intellectual and sub-intellectual world. He might embark on his renewed reflections by noting that our contemporary distinction between philosophy and theology was not of his making and should be largely repudiated as a medieval mistake: serious theologians build on what philosophers have achieved and serious philosophers recognize the limitations of their enterprise – and refrain from trying to conceal these limitations by reductionist accounts of the world they are attempting to understand: the device not of philosophers, but of sophists or propagandists. On this (Platonic) distinction neo-Augustine – normally hereinafter 'our Augustine' – will want to comment.

In his earlier incarnation Augustine had argued in *The City of God* (for example, at 10.9) that exaggerated claims to philosophical completeness had infected the genuine metaphysical successes of the Platonists of his day and led such as Porphyry into superstition:

For even Porphyry promises a certain kind of purification of the soul by means of theurgy. His argument is, however, developed hesitantly and with shame.... You may see, indeed, that his opinion vacillates between two alternatives: the crime of sacrilegious curiosity and the profession of philosophy. (Dyson's translation)

He will add that in the twenty-first century such superstition – such 'sacrilegious curiosity' – often reappears as some form of scientism.

Our Augustine will follow his third-century Christian predecessor Origen (*Against Celsus* 4.62-70) in arguing that what we now call 'theology' can go beyond what we now call 'philosophy' because it has access to further data – derived from revelation, yet intelligible, even empirically intelligible, when so derived – for describing the human condition and for reflection upon it. Such data could in the first instance be treated by non-theists as allowing for the possibility of various thought -experiments, but it will turn out to be more than mere material for such experiments if it appears to resolve – and to be the only possible way to resolve – an expanding set of major problems which the honest philosopher has to admit remain without solution in what are now thought of as strictly 'philosophical' terms. Thus, Augustine would claim, from 'philosophy' we can move to advanced philosophy (that is, theology), just as in science we can move (*inter alia*) from Euclidean to non-Euclidean geometry, and we can demonstrate that such a move really does add to our understanding of the immense complexity of ourselves and our world, and immeasurably more than the limitations of the so-called sciences.

Our Augustine's project in the twenty-first century, as I have thus evoked it, would differ from that of many, indeed most, contemporary theologians in several significant respects which can best be understood historically, and an historical approach will reveal the sort of theology our Augustine would have in mind in the twenty-first century as substantially different from what now passes muster under that name.

The third-century Alexandrian Origen seems to have been the first Christian to have attempted a full-blown theological account of the universe, but by the Middle Ages such projects were accepted as part, indeed as goal, of a Christian intellectual life, often taking the form, as with Thomas Aquinas, of a *Summa*, an attentive and considered summary of what we have learned thus far in theological enquiry. Such *Summas* consist of philosophical reflection on philosophical ideas derived from all available sources and on data generated by Church tradition and the Christian and Jewish scriptures. Great stress would be placed on the opinions of weighty Christian (and soon also pagan) authorities: Augustine himself above all. Truth, not smart-ass originality, would be the overriding aim.

Yet even within that seemingly harmonious medieval intellectual universe, apparently capable of being further developed within more or less clearly defined parameters, lay seeds of discord, and nowhere would that become more apparent than in ethics. Its sources were legion, but one of the most obvious – to us now and to some few even then – was the clash between Aristotle's account of virtue and Augustine's emphasis on God's grace and the impossibility of perfection in our present life. Naturally, the clash was formulated more stridently in that Augustine was a Christian bishop, while Aristotle could be written off (well before Luther) as 'that pagan'. How, asked such as Peter of John Olivi, Thomas Bradwardine and Gregory of Rimini, can the views of a pre-Christian master be taught while in the Schools we hear nothing about grace? And it must be admitted that no medieval thinker succeeded in reconciling with a full-blooded Pauline Christianity the 'Aristotle' they cited – even interpreted in the spirit of the Neoplatonism of his late Greek commentators as a believer in God as efficient cause and with a providentialist attitude to human beings – a portrait that would have surprised Augustine, not to speak of many other Patristic writers, the majority of whom think of Aristotle as an atheist precisely in that he ignores any such providence.

Already in the thirteenth century the Arts Faculty of the University of Paris felt entitled to present Aristotle with little anxiety about his apparently unchristian features. That might be bad enough, and indeed reprehensible, but when the problem cropped up unambiguously in Faculties of Theology, the ticking bomb was eventually going to explode, spasmodic expulsions of 'heretics' notwithstanding. Even if some would argue – and I am not one of them – that the supposed confusion of Aristotle with 'Christianity' (as if we all knew what that is!) had been sorted out in the High Middle Ages, that was not how it appeared in the early sixteenth century.

Hence Luther (and he was not alone) began to think that his time was misspent lecturing on Aristotle's ethics, as by then was part of the 'tradition': so much the worse, the more radical clergy began to think, for the tradition! What was required was an insistence that the undoubted word of God in the Bible – so understandable to those willing to think hard about it! – must always take precedence over such traditions in the Church. And with that axiom agreed, it became easy to believe that far more traditions and habits of the Church were unbiblical than had as yet been recognized. Thus, for example, metaphysics should be largely replaced by exegesis (That might even sound Augustinian). The dispute had reached the stage of being about the essence of Christianity itself. Everyone claimed to know what that is, and many were asking themselves whether followers of the 'Anti-Christ of Rome' could really be Christians at all. After all, as is still often bruited, Augustine's ideas about sex, predestination and original sin caused much of the Western malaise from which we are now happily liberating ourselves!

Tradition – any kind of tradition, but especially the ecclesiastical variety – had by now for many become an idol – a sacred cow – to be gunned down. So in what later would in some jurisdictions be called faculties of Divinity – as distinct from backward-looking and more 'traditional' faculties of Theology – what used to be wider theological enquiry was substantially restricted to study of the Word of God in Scripture. And initially it was assumed – not least by Luther who was horrified when he found that the opposite was the case, and must surely be put down to diabolical intervention – that the free Christian man – freed, that is, from fallible human masters – would readily recognize *the* right and godly interpretation of biblical texts. Which did not happen; rather in matters of interpretation every man had the opportunity to be his own pope, while the larger of the new groups – originally Lutherans and Calvinists, though the numbers soon multiplied – formed their own more or less organized and standardized teaching traditions in university departments that were rivals to the older Catholic 'houses of study'. As a Lutheran, like Shakespeare's Horatio, you could go to Wittenberg, just as a Catholic could still go to the University of Paris or – if perhaps his traditionalism was more radical – to one of the newer Jesuit foundations.

And thus more or less it remained till the end of the eighteenth and beginning of the nineteenth centuries when a second paradigm shift occurred for two not unrelated reasons. The first was ever-growing hostility to the Bible, especially in France, and to the Old Testament in particular, as presenting us with a god whose morals fall well below 'enlightened' human standards. Already since Patristic times certain Old Testament passages had apparently required defence by wildly convoluted theorizing: such are the sacrifice of Isaac or God's command to Hosea to marry a prostitute, not to speak of the use of other prostitutes to promote Israelite military successes. You could resort to a more or less unregulated use of allegory to disembarrass yourself of morally difficult passages, and by the fourteenth century a highly sophisticated casuistry had been developed, not least by the increasingly popular Duns Scotus, to explain away such apparently obvious moral anomalies.

By the eighteenth century, the spread of avowed atheism was much encouraged by a Christian inability to explain God's seemingly immoral behaviour on behalf of a trivial little people often set, as under Joshua, on genocide: a practice, of course, widely favoured and enacted by many in antiquity. At a time of growing demand for the reform of barbarous European penal codes – here the efforts of Voltaire were significant and effective – continuing respect for barbarous religious texts shocked those of enlightened sensibilities: we might compare the revulsion of some contemporary Muslims to the barbarities advocated in the Qur'an and practised – not least against Jews – by the Prophet himself.

Something had to be done about the Bible if Christianity – in the first instance Protestant Christianity since Protestants had no other source of belief – was to survive, not least in Protestant Prussia where Frederick the Great was the first radically to liberalize the penal code. That something – that second factor in the paradigm shift – came, perhaps 'providentially' (at least in the longer run), from the beginnings of what we now know as 'classical philology', the pioneering work in which was Friedrich Wolff's *Prolegomenon to the Study of Homer* in the 1770s.

The work of Wolff and his successors, above all their attempts to set ancient texts in their historical context, was revolutionary in many ways, but above all in revealing that texts, especially very ancient texts, can grow over time, so that the modern reader can now recognize in, say, the text of Homer, earlier and later layers blended together in the version he or she now reads. Such an approach was to reveal, for example, that some parts of Homer had been 'cleaned up' over time, while others remained more primitive, so indicating the nature of older versions of the stories. In the *Odyssey* the hero unashamedly searches for poison for his arrows, while in the more

bowdlerized *Iliad* there is no use of poison arrows on either side –
though in one place, after the combat between Menelaus and Paris
(*Iliad* 4.150ff.), the excessive concern about what seems a trivial
wound suffered by Menelaus probably indicates that the original
version recorded poison arrows being openly accepted and widely
used.

Philological techniques of this sort were originally developed
for the interpretation of secular classical texts, but they could also
be applied to the Bible, especially to those Old Testament passages
seemingly vulnerable on moral grounds: that is, we can recognize
that in such passages we find not literally the words of God or of one
of his prophetic mouthpieces so much as records of the gradually
growing awareness by the Jewish people of God's nature, as they
came to see it as less 'primitive' than their own primitive forefathers
had supposed. So far so good! Late eighteenth-century Christians,
and especially Protestant Christians, had been let off the hook! But
the price they would have to pay for their release was higher – and
more demanding – than they could have originally supposed.

There is an important and obvious difference between the Old
Testament and the New: the former was composed over hundreds
of years, the latter over less than a hundred. It might thus look easy
to argue that the new philology, which had moved from classical
to biblical studies, would work primarily and conveniently for the
Old Testament, which could be regarded as a body of cumulative
evidence for the growing sophistication of Jewish ideas of God
and of God's intentions for mankind. Thus, we might interpret the
story of the sacrifice of Isaac as showing that in early days the Jews,
like other Semitic peoples, such as the Carthaginians in historical
times, practised human sacrifice, not least of (first-born) children.
Eventually, so the interpretation would run, the Jews realized that
God wanted first no human sacrifice, then (at least some supposed)
no blood -sacrifice at all but rather the 'sacrifice' of a pure heart.

So far – again – so good, but the earliest parts of the *New* Testament
were composed at least twenty years after the death of Jesus, and
the New Testament canon was not (more or less) fixed until the
latter part of the second century. What might have happened during
those critical years between the thirties and the late fifties of the
first century A.D.? There could be redactions, developed versions,
Midrash and suchlike embroidering of the original accounts of
Jesus. At least we should expect to find substantially disputed

interpretations of the sacred text, some of which might be quite radical, especially in the Protestant world where, as we have noted, there was always something of a sense that each man can interpret the text as he sees fit: where 'tradition' is of scarce help to him, being reduced to little more than other men's guesses.

Even without the obvious abuses of form-criticism of the New Testament – by which, for example, it can be supposed that if the text appears in a linguistically stylized form, then the events it purports to describe are unlikely to be historical and are in some undefined sense only metaphorically or spiritually informative: even without that, it is clear that the deconstructing of both Testaments, beginning as early as Machiavelli, passed through Hobbes and Spinoza to attain to new excesses in the nineteenth century and has continued ever since, so ensuring that Protestant theology can enjoy no secure confidence in its only bastion – that is, the Testaments both Old and New – while where Catholics follow Protestant biblical techniques like sheep – and even without any reference to 'tradition' – their 'theology' will finish up – often has finished up – in the same place as Protestant 'divinity'. That does not mean that our only remaining choices are between an ignorantly fundamentalist Scriptural interpretation and atheism (or agnosticism), but at least that an account of the development of Christian doctrine must start with an account of the development of the Bible texts themselves.

Such, in very broad outline, is the 'spiritual' world into which our twenty-first-century Augustine will arrive. He will find that for many theologians their subject has become the name of a 'discipline' in search of a subject-matter, and that there now exists a strong tendency to view what is left of traditional Christianity as a kind of non-governmental organization – though why anyone should want it so seems to be a philosophical (or psychological) rather than a theological problem. Augustine will certainly have to discuss that as part of his reply to our contemporary atheists, and he will have to affirm that a merely do-gooding 'theology' will not serve his Catholic turn – even though there is obviously nothing amiss about doing good as such!

And our Augustine will have to continue by observing that although most contemporary theology has deprived itself of the tools with which to offer any kind of interesting response to the non-theistic features of modern culture, he must therefore return to (and defend) a good deal more of both 'tradition' and the historical Bible (*ad litteram* is how he would put it) than contemporary theologians would now normally dare to propose; for they have abandoned their posts along with those scriptural and traditional beliefs on the sole basis of which those 'posts' seemed worth defending.

*

In the first seven chapters of this book Augustine will say little about contemporary 'theology' and theologians, though he will show as he proceeds that he understands the need to tell a more substantial, less impressionistic theological story than most theologians now think necessary or even possible, for their judgements have been formed by a systemically developed ignorance of the history of theology. In these chapters he will indicate that his philosophical arguments, contextualized in much older and half-forgotten 'philosophical' and 'theological' beliefs, can call to account many of our own culture's sacred cows. Then in Chapter 8 he will turn directly to contemporary theological trends and practices, to point to the minimum specifically *intellectual* work required if the discipline of 'theology' (as distinct from 'philosophy') is to be saved from the contempt in which (except in head-in-sand quarters) it is now almost universally held. His aim will be to replace secular idols (whether or not worshipped by quisling theologians) by something surprisingly like the thoughtful 'theological' Christianity he preached even to the uneducated in the early fifth-century North African city of Hippo.

In presenting Augustine's 'current' views I would not wish to argue that he would disown the *better* theological thought that has appeared since the fifth century, not least among the more philosophical – thus of less strict observance – of the Thomists. He will, however, argue that much of this thought is presented in too arid, too abstract, too systematic, too 'generalizing', too impersonal, almost (one might say) too unliterary and too unspiritual a form to do what it seeks to do – above all when it seeks to talk not to itself or to those few of its remaining adherents who actually *think* about what they espouse, but *to* – and insofar as possible without intellectual compromises, *in the language of* – more contemporary debaters. He will not, however, concede that renewed debate should be conducted on the basis of a set of assumptions presupposed by opponents of Christianity, or insinuated by political correctness –

often recognizable at its most toxic among 'theologians' – and thus ab initio fatal to Christian claims! Indeed, he will repeatedly argue that it is the very axioms and assumptions of much contemporary philosophical talk that are easiest for him to challenge!

In the first two chapters, our Augustine will briefly set out the principles that govern his moral world and discuss the significance he attaches to his own unique individual life and to the parallel and unique lives of others. We shall then be in a position to let him loose on the twenty-first century – though he knows and will confess that in moving in our contemporary world he must admit to a number of errors he himself has made (and assumed himself likely to make) in his earthly lifetime. He will point some of these out as he goes along, for, as he himself has said, if you read my works in chronological order you will see the development of my mind (*Reconsiderations*, prologue 3); or again, in *On the Trinity* (1.1.5, [Hill's translation]):

> If anyone reads this work and says, 'I understand what is being said but it is not true', he is at liberty to affirm his own conviction and refute mine if he can. If he succeeds in doing so charitably and truthfully, and also takes the trouble to let me know…, then that would be the choicest plum that could fall to me from these labours of mine.

Or again, in *Against Two Letters of the Pelagians* 2.5:

> It is part of a Catholic disposition to express willingness to accept correction if one is mistaken.

Criticize me where I am wrong, that is, but do me the justice to read carefully what I have said. Looking back from the twenty-first century, he will observe wryly that much criticism has been aimed at him by those who have scarce opened his books!

A final caveat: in the present book some will claim to 'find' that I am pushing my own views and attributing them to Augustine. Certainly, I agree with most of what I attribute to an Augustine returning to confront the twenty-first century: that is because I am impressed by the contemporaneity of Augustine's thought and not because I am thereby attempting to lend my own views a spurious authority. What I attribute to Augustine is no more than positions

I believe he would defend if he wished substantially to re-present his own powerfully developed teachings, while updating them to face new and unforeseen challenges. Hence, I believe that what follows in the present study is a legitimate, coherent and intelligible correction and expansion of his original views in light of ideas as yet unavailable, even at times inconceivable, in the fifth century of the Christian era.

In his own day Augustine argued with dissident Christians and with pagans. Nowadays few would call themselves 'pagans', though many would be happy to be called 'secularists'. Our Augustine might see scant conceptual difference between the content of the two terms, for the secularists have their 'gods' (their idols) too, albeit they do not so designate them: their rights, their 'charismatic' politicians, their celebs and their 'autonomy'. Throughout the following narrative Augustine will make little distinction between pagans and secularists when treating of recent centuries; indeed, he will view our age as in many respects a reversion to some of the least attractive and least defensible aspects of ancient paganism.

1

The Foundations of Augustine's Moral Empiricism: Truth, Love and Sin

Thomas Aquinas began his masterwork of philosophical and biblical theology by offering a set of proofs for the existence of God. There is nothing like that in Augustine, though more informal arguments for God's existence are to be found in his writings. In the most famous of these he observes that his proof is fragile (HR, 2.15.39), depending as it does on the Neoplatonic claim that if something can be shown to be 'higher' than the human mind, it must exist in God's mind, and that since truth is higher than the human mind, God must exist.

We cannot account for this difference between Augustine and Aquinas merely by noting that Augustine had no need to prove God's existence since atheists in our modern sense of the word were all but unknown in antiquity, the word being normally applied not to someone who denied the existence of a god or gods, but to someone who held that gods have no interest in the affairs of mortals, being too blessed to be bothered with them: that is, an ancient 'atheist' was normally a denier of divine providence, not of the existence of divinity. Augustine tells us in the *Confessions* (6.5.7; 7.7.11) that he was never seriously troubled by the thought of God's non-existence; what matters is not God's existence but his nature.

Anselm, who was Aquinas's predecessor in raising the spectre of the modern-style atheist, wants to confirm the Psalmist's view that he is a fool, even though his arguments and concerns too are less about proving that God must exist than about showing what sort of being a providential God infinitely removed from ourselves must be. Indeed, although in offering his Five Ways to demonstrate God's existence Aquinas appears to follow in what he supposed to be Anselm's footsteps, both of them still lived in a world where self-styled atheists remained all but unknown. Then why did Aquinas feel the necessity to offer arguments for God's existence, let alone start his major treatise with them? Perhaps because some of his Muslim predecessors had done something similar, though that merely pushes the question a stage further back to why did *they* offer arguments for the existence of God (rather than of just one God), and why did Aquinas decide to follow suit, thus adopting a methodology very different from that of Augustine, his main Christian source apart from the Scriptures? Perhaps being a tidy, system-building man with a university job he wanted to start from the foundations of his physical, moral and spiritual universe, before proceeding to build on those foundations.

Augustine was not a tidy man with a university job – nor does he write like one; nor did he have any particular desire to construct hopefully watertight philosophical systems, though he was willing to learn from the more systematic thinking of others, whether pagans like Plotinus or Christians like Origen. He seems also to have thought that metaphysical mistakes, not least disbelief in God, are rooted less in bad thinking than in special pleading evoked by morally perverse desires (JG, 106.17.4; Ps, 53 (52) 2, etc.) inhibiting our recognition of the obvious and impelling a rationalizing construction of a world in which our own behaviour can be justified, or at least not condemned. In that he may have had a point: we learn to rationalize almost as soon as we learn to think, and since hard thinking is troublesome, rationalizing may seem more useful, certainly more attractive, especially if it allays pangs of conscience and licenses us to do 'as we like' – or to feel justified if we do what other people, with good reason, don't like. The habit goes back to Adam and Eve who, humanly enough, wanted to excuse themselves: not me, Gov.! Fallen *angels* may seem – especially to poets – more heroic; they have no one else to incriminate.

If Augustine does not begin with God, what is his starting point? Usually, something that has come to puzzle him: Why do people – Manichaeans – think there are two principles in the universe, a good and a bad? Why do others – Pelagians – suppose that in this life we can be perfect? Why do others – Sceptics – think that I cannot be sure that I exist? Why do we suppose that some pleasures are illicit? Why do we suppose there some things we *ought* to do, or at least ought to want to do? Answers to such questions may lead to belief in God, but the questions themselves could occur to anyone, believer or unbeliever, learned or illiterate, introvert or extrovert, genius or fool. They 'occur': we 'bump into' them as we fill in (or fill out) our lives. When we bump into them, we cannot but reflect on them, however minimally and however much we try to ignore them or make assumptions based on other people's views on them.

And as we thus reflect, we also 'bump into' recurrent explanatory principles. Many of us will share some of the principles prominent in the mind of Augustine, probably for the simple reason that, being like him human, we can do no other. So if we ask where Augustine starts, we are also asking what principles he notes in reflecting on those questions that regularly puzzled him. And we find that constantly he reverts to three particular themes in various guises: truth, love and sin. He will be surprised to find that many of our contemporaries disparage reflection on the last of these as obscurantism. When he thinks about these themes, he is both looking at the world – looking, that is, at what his experiences tell him is going on 'out there' – and trying to sort out his experience in the light of whatever learning he has at his disposal or can access. The experience itself – with the empirically acquired data – comes first, and philosophical or theological explanations or constructions may follow. Inability to find such explanations or constructions *empirically* may push him to accept views of philosophers or philosophical theologians who offer a further dimension of reality through which to 'come to terms' with his own experiences and better understand those of others.

Since I intend in the present book to update Augustine's moral and spiritual universe, it will reveal how his understanding of truth, love and sin works itself out in the contemporary *human* sphere. Although truth will govern his wider reflections – as explanations of the universe as a whole – he will for now introduce such larger questions only insofar as they impinge on or follow from more immediately moral, political and spiritual concerns. He will start by explaining where he finds in the world and in himself the three themes – truth, love and sin – that reveal the parameters of his moral universe and will eventually lead him beyond it. With such a foundation, I can have him intervene as student and critic of twenty-first-century moral, political and spiritual thinking.

But why moral, political *and* spiritual – and Augustine could add aesthetic – when the title of the present chapter speaks only of his *moral* empiricism? The answer is that for Augustine there is little difference between the moral and the spiritual. We are reminded that there is no word in Latin which translates our concept of 'moral', and thus for Augustine both 'moral' and 'spiritual' relate to how one lives – 'moral' presumably referring primarily to basic behaviour – but both requiring God's grace. And insofar as 'aesthetic' refers to what is beautiful or fine, that too is part of the same agglomerate. Our word 'aesthetics' – with its corresponding subject -matter – was coined in the eighteenth century; in ancient times aesthetics was part of ethics (or vice versa). Augustine will note that that observation is true not only of Christian but also of pagan thinkers.

Such preliminaries cleared away, Augustine can turn to his account of truth, leaving aside, at least for the moment, his identification of Truth with Christ and remaining within the more secular-seeming domain that is appropriate to his first steps into our twenty-first century. But as we recognized in the Introduction, unlike most Christian thinkers of his day, Augustine was not a Greek-speaking but a Latin-speaking bishop who read most of his Greek philosophy through Latin sources or through translations into Latin. That his culture was Latin, and typically so, meant that in tandem with his professional knowledge of Cicero as the master of oratory, he was familiar with Cicero, the reporter of philosophical themes more or less unknown to Greek-speaking bishops: in particular of debates between Stoics and Sceptics about the possibility of knowledge. What he learned of Scepticism from Cicero coloured Augustine's thought throughout his life, but perhaps even more basic was his first enthusiasm for philosophy, aroused by a reading of Cicero's now largely lost *Hortensius*, a text based on an earlier work of Aristotle's urging its readers to think philosophically and to enjoy doing so.

All the major pagan philosophical schools (except obviously the Sceptics, but including Augustine's favoured Platonists) had a 'thick' account of knowledge; that is, they thought of knowledge in much the same way as do many of our contemporaries insofar as they want to link it with certainty. Augustine learned not only not to share that view, but to find it unnecessary in the search for truth, as well as contrary to ordinary human experience. For there are but few 'facts' about reality which we can 'know' indubitably: such are truths of logic as that either p or not-p must be the case (AS, 3.10.23), or of mathematics, or of what we think we sense (3.11.26), or arguably of our own existence. We can 'know' nothing of the past, whether our own or more general history. Although we can know we exist, we have only limited knowledge of what we are like, or of what we will be tomorrow (S, 340A.8) – that is, how we will behave tomorrow – for our 'hearts are an abyss' (Ps, 42 (43).13); we are a great deep (C, 4.14.22). Above all, we do not know or understand our own motives, since we are divided.

I must gather myself together, Augustine tells us in the *Confessions* (2.1.1), for the dispersal of my affections 'tore me apart when I turned away from you, the only Unity, and lost myself in multiplicity', for (as so often happens), 'It is I who willed it, and I who did not – the same I' (C, 8.10.22). For Augustine this last reflection is morally basic, not least because it reminds us that we have memories of certain truths which we now see only through a glass darkly: of happiness (HR, 2.9.26), of goodness and human nature (T, 8.3-4; 13.1.2), of the just law which, as Paul had said, is impressed on the human heart (T, 14.15.21) and even of God who may 'illuminate' what we think.

It does not matter whether we have *knowledge* of past events because we can get on very well if we can find reliable and authoritative witnesses to historicity. Thus (and in the absence of DNA testing – and in each case if he has no reason to doubt their veracity) Augustine knows from his mother who his father is, and he can check with midwives or other relevant witnesses who his mother is (UB, 12.26). With historical events more generally we place the same reliance on intelligible and informed authorities. Certainly, if we have only one source of information and that source is confused, it is not reliable; but if it is coherent and especially if its testimony is supported by that of others, it would be irrational not to accept it.

In such cases scepticism is the irrational option; we have no reason – to use Augustine's own example – to deny that Cicero executed the Catilinarian conspirators in 63 B.C. (UB, 11.25):

though 'Not only do I not know it, but I am quite certain I do not know it'. Similarly, we have no reason to deny that Hitler died in 1945, though no one now living saw him dead and the location of whatever remains of his body is unknown (thanks to Stalin). Beliefs in religion are essentially no different: we believe the account of the life of Jesus which the Scriptures which the Church has accepted describe, and the continuing Church bears witness to their veracity.

And as in the case of Jesus, Augustine never makes the mistake of supposing that because we 'know' a number of useful facts about a person or object or event, we know all about them in the sense that we have fully 'captured' their essential being. That sort of claim is what his account of confirmed belief is intended to reject. In treating of such belief he thinks 'Stoically' of assenting – thus to believe is to think with assent (PRS, 2.5) – but he declines to follow the Stoics (and some modern post-Fregeans) in thinking or assuming that all knowledge is propositional, and that what we 'know' is just whatever propositions we are entitled to assent to. He would have more sympathy with Saul Kripke's 'rigid designator': that is, we 'capture' enough truth about the thing to which we refer to be able to speak intelligibly about it in specific (and linguistically shared) contexts.

There is further an experiential, first-hand knowledge of a type Augustine would have learned to recognize from the Platonists – had he needed philosophical teachers to tell him what is a matter of non-philosophical common sense. When, according to Plato or Plotinus, we recognize the Good, we are not assenting to a proposition that there is a Good (though we may do that as well); we are accepting that we can 'see' it, that in some way we are acquainted with it. We also know that however many true propositions we can formulate about it, we shall precisely *not* be able to 'capture' it. Nor is it only in the case of metaphysical items like the Good that we meet and 'recognize' only relevant characteristics. Augustine knows who his friend Alypius is, but, eschewing reductionism, he would never suppose that – although various propositions are true or false about Alypius – the man himself could be broken down into a set of qualities each of which could be described propositionally. Yes, Alypius lived in North Africa and not in Australia. Perhaps he was partly Berber, but he was certainly not Aborigine. Yet, however many true propositions can be well formed about Alypius (or anyone else), they can never be exhaustive.

There is an unusual but notable corollary to Augustine's account of 'cognitive' experience, that is, his version of knowledge by 'acquaintance': a darker sort of limited but debased 'acquaintance' with – even 'love' of – objects, or of persons treated as objects. Thus we can be acquainted with human beings as vulnerable and exploitable:

> We ought not to love human beings in the sense in which one hears gourmets say 'I love thrushes'. Why not? Because the gourmet loves to kill and consume. When he says that he loves thrushes, he loves them so that they may not exist, so that he may destroy them....We should obviously not love human beings as things to be consumed. (JE, 8.5)

Augustine regards his awareness of the significance of the first-person experience of human individuals as peculiarly Christian, but he knows that his philosophical account of it is greatly influenced by Platonism. He connects it to the distinction between knowledge and understanding, or between learning and wisdom. Greeks since the time of Heraclitus – that is, well before Plato – knew that much learning does not add up to good sense, while Augustine's Latin distinguishes between *scientia* (knowledge) and *sapientia* (wisdom) – words often invoked by his interpreters as terms of art. His account of 'understanding' is careful to note that the illumination of God gives us the ability to do much more than 'parrot' bits of information (C 10.7.11).

In the Platonic tradition right back to Plato himself – especially to the *Republic* – we learn of a special kind of knowledge available to morally, spiritually and intellectually trained and focused individuals: knowledge, that is, of the Form of the Good. The nature of that Good may be expanded and our understanding of it further developed (though Plato himself could hardly have expanded it in a Christian direction since he views it as more or less impersonal). Be that as it may, according to any sort of platonizing theory it is impossible to *know* the Good – we might better say 'understand', or 'comprehend' (at least something of) the Good – without also *loving* the Good, and so desiring urgently to have it in mind whenever we are acting as specifically human agents. For the Good is productive of itself: such that if you love it, you want to share it as something valuable and admirable within the society in which you live. Insofar as you know it, you will love it, not by inference but in the very experience of knowing it:

> Give me a man who yearns, give me a man who is hungry, give me a man travelling in the desert, who is thirsty and sighing for the spring of the eternal country. Give me that sort of man; he knows what I mean. But if I talk to a cold man, he does not know what I am talking about. (JG, 26.4)

Plato's view of such sharing – itself shared by Augustine – is immensely plausible, as well as informative about the nature of goodness itself: If I see a beautiful work of art, or watch a beautiful sunset, and if someone says to me, 'Would you want your family and friends – or any wider group – to see these things?' I would reply (that is, if I loved them or even merely respected them), 'Well, of course I would'. Hence, in the Platonic tradition, to which at least thus far Augustine subscribes, to love something in the 'best' or 'strictest' sense of the word 'love' entails wanting to share whatever is lovable with others (insofar as it is good for them and for yourself to do so). The caveat is important: Augustine explained in HR (1.3.6) that he had no time for 'wife-swapping', doubtless believing that here the golden rule does not apply since its application would do no good to any of the parties involved. Of course, in the case of Beauty itself, which is God, as distinct from mere earthly beauties, the inspiration and consequent generosity are unbounded:

> We have that which we can all enjoy equally and in common. In her there is no straitness, no deficiency. All the lovers she receives are altogether free of jealousy of one another; she is shared by all in common and chaste to each. None says to another: 'Stand back that I too may approach' or 'Take your hands off that I may embrace her too'. All cleave to the same thing. Her food is not divided individually and you do not drink anything that I cannot drink too. From that common store you can convert nothing to your private possession. (HR, 2.14.37)

In the pagan Platonic tradition envy had always been a curiously ungodly characteristic. In complementary vein, and in the same tradition, it is impossible to love fully without having some more or less explicit comprehension of what it is that one loves. Indeed,

Augustine thinks (as does Plato) that we are born with just such an implicit desire and comprehension that human viciousness and sophistry will seek to extirpate. His mother Monnica is depicted in *The Happy Life* and elsewhere as a simple soul whose underlying goodness has remained uncorrupted. Indeed, without a certain residue of such basic goodness, we should be left only with various lusts such as Plato attributes to his 'tyrannical man'. That lust, which Augustine summarizes as the 'lust for domination', is to control and manipulate not only the bodies but also, diabolically (CG 4.4; *On Music* 6.13.41), the minds and even the souls of other people. Augustine, of course, is far from intending to imply that we should decline to *instruct* other people; instruction properly is neither manipulation nor domination, albeit sophists may present it as such, even by urging that the immature should be left uninstructed so as to be 'free' to work things out for themselves. We shall return to such 'freedom' and Augustine's criticism of it later, especially in Chapters 3 and 8, merely noticing here that those who object (for example) to parents 'imposing' a religion on their children show no such concern about imposing their own language, and therefore, to no insignificant degree, their cultural habits and ideological preferences.

Augustine has already moved from the first of his principles – truth – to the second, which appears inseparable from it: that is, to love. But his account of love, though, as we have seen, expressed, in its philosophical formulations, in Platonic language, is again proposed as a Christian adaptation *and correction* of Plato. And he will propose corrections even more radical when he shifts from a 'Platonic' metaphysic of the Good to Platonic accounts of human nature and of the possibilities of human perfectibility. Then he will argue that much 'Prometheanism' – notions of the perfecting and even the trans-humanization of man – are a grotesque distortion of some of the least accurate and least intelligible parts of Plato's account of human nature.

If we look at the history of Platonism since the time of Plato himself, we notice that down to the third century A.D. members of the school believed (as did virtually all Greco-Roman thinkers) that whatever perfection is possible for human beings is possible in the present life and can be achieved without divine assistance. Those of Augustine's ancient opponents known as Pelagians clung to a modified version of the same idea: according to Pelagius, with our baptism God has given us the last of the tools we need to perfect ourselves. How easy is it to see, our contemporary Augustine will tell us, why a secularized version of Pelagian ideas is popular among those hoping to construct a *crude* harmony between the Enlightenment and Christianity. Pelagius's account of the origin of the soul – shared by many ancient Christians, but not by Augustine – was that each soul is created by God and 'inserted' as a separate substance into our inherited and corrupt bodies. That contradicts the sound Augustinian thesis (CG, 14.3) that the body is regularly corrupted by the soul, not *vice versa*.

Of course, Plato and the pagan Platonists subscribed to a much stronger version of a rather similar idea, of which many early Christians – most notoriously Origen – accepted a key element: namely that our souls pre-exist our bodies and have 'fallen' into them, or been sent down into them for re-education after sin. Indeed in circulation was an even stronger version, more obviously impossible for 'orthodox' Christians – and recognized as such at least from the time of Justin Martyr in the second century – namely that our souls are immortal by their very nature: not, that is, simply *created* immortal by God. But if the soul is naturally immortal, then the Platonic notion that we should attain 'likeness to God' – which goes back to four passages of Plato himself – should have been interpreted differently by ancient pagans and Christians (though Christians were often confused about what it originally meant). Plato's version, still nominally defended by Plotinus in the third century of our era, was that attaining likeness to God is not a matter of becoming immortal (for by nature we are immortal already), but of attaining goodness, knowledge and pure love: pre-eminent characteristics of divine beings.

It follows from any notion of our native immortality that we can and therefore must work out our own perfection; hence in our twenty-first century Augustine will propose strong objections to the logically connected idea that 'ought' implies 'can'; this will appear in Chapter 3. As for the Platonists, Plotinus formulates the genuinely Platonic idea of human capacity with exemplary clarity; those who think they need divine assistance to attain perfection and the happy vision of the good life – some sort of unification with God – are, frankly, morally lazy (*Ennead 3.2.9*). As we have noted, that strong form of the 'Pelagian' challenge, propped up by the claim that we are immortal by nature, was always recognized by ancient Christians – even those markedly platonizing like Justin – as radically incompatible with their core beliefs. It did not take an Augustine to work that much out, though it did take an Augustine to imply that Pelagius was too close to the pagan view.

In antiquity Plotinus was the last, even among the pagans, to hold so challenging a position. His pupil Porphyry began to hesitate, to sit on the fence. *His* pupil Iamblichus went the whole hog, thus setting the stage for the last days of ancient Platonism in this regard. By then we are seen as incapable of attaining perfection unaided and needing what they called 'theurgy', a kind of pagan sacramentalism normally misconstrued by ancient Christians as a magical attempt to manipulate the gods. Such a 'paradigm shift' among the pagans seems, perhaps surprisingly, to have had no immediate connection with the growing influence of Christianity; the very fact that Plotinus mentions the problem suggests that many, even of the more intellectual pagans, were beginning to have their doubts about human moral capacity. Those doubts seem part of what is often referred to (originally by E. R. Dodds in his once well-known study entitled *The Greeks and the Irrational*) as a 'failure of nerve' among late Greco-Roman thinkers, though whether it was a failure of nerve or a recognition of reality is obviously debatable: Augustine would settle for the second option. 'So far, so good'! The debate is still very much ongoing.

For after antiquity, and so long as Platonists remained at least minimally Christian – as did the group assembled in Marsilio Ficino's fifteenth-century Florentine Academy – they had to remember – and just about managed it – that man is not immortal by nature: that he both needs and desires at least some measure – this even Pelagius would allow – of ongoing divine assistance. Yet, ironically, Ficino's associates exalted human capacity and cosmic significance in a way that even Plotinus would have considered exaggerated, indeed as more or less Gnostic.

When 'Platonism' was finally 'emancipated' from 'parochial' (that is, Jewish) Christianity, it often re-appeared in 'Romantic' guise in the late eighteenth and early nineteenth century – sometimes combined with a rather Stoic-seeming nature-mysticism or pantheism. Then, however, it gave opening not just to a Renaissance exaltation of man within a still minimally Christian framework – signally an attempted correction of medieval (and Reformed) excesses in projecting an image of man so debased as hardly to remain an image of God at all – but to the Prometheanism of the Enlightenment, the Romantics and ultimately Nietzsche. Much of the exuberance of the Romantic debasement of Plato was to give way to the weary realism – it would be misleading to say neo-Augustinianism – of such post-Romantics as Flaubert and Proust. The final stage (or nadir) of the merely Romantic figure is the banal and debased Madame Bovary (not to speak of her continuing, indeed potentially endless, stream of literary and more recently cinematic and televisual successors).

Yet in recounting this history our Augustine will tell us that we have almost lost sight of both the Platonic and the non-Platonic aspects of his account of love – albeit in the light of much subsequent religious reflection we can be pardoned for so doing. Nevertheless, he will insist that the dispute between Christians and 'classical' Platonists about human capacities is important, not least because it affects the proper evaluation of that love designated by the Greek word *eros*.

Eros was originally viewed as a passion, often of a dangerous sort, and regularly referred to by classical poets as an infection from which one should keep one's distance, and which, if contracted, requires some kind of medical cure. Yet, as Augustine well knew, that exalted and dangerous power is precisely what endears it to the Platonists. For it alone gives us the strength to rise above the finite and, in a kind of passionate 'madness' – Plato's word in the *Phaedrus* (244a–245c) – to advance to the infinite: to progress from what Plato identifies in the *Republic* as the world of 'becoming' and even from merely finite 'being', to that which is 'beyond finite being': that is, to the Good itself, the source of existence of all else and means by which that existence can alone be comprehended.

Like the Christians (and many classical Greeks as far back as the time of Hesiod, that is in the eighth century B.C.) Plato tells us that we are a fallen race. What indeed is the difference between a Platonic soul and a god, except that, for whatever reason, the gods are not 'fallen'? Yet he seems comparatively uninterested in the mechanics of what he presumably regarded as a metaphysical event as much as an historical fact. Yet if concentration on metaphysics allows Plato to avoid reflection on an 'historical' fall of man, no such escape clause is on offer in the Jewish and Christian Bible, at least as read in antiquity.

Adam and Eve fell – so it was eventually agreed – in historical time: a view that entailed explaining not only how the fall occurred but also the effects it has on our 'erotic' power to advance to the Good itself. In that latter respect our Augustine will repeat that his divergence from the pagans – let alone from our contemporary 'progressives' – is as unambiguous as ever. We retain the desire to return, and the desire for Goodness ever haunts us, but we lack the capacity to secure what we need, desire, indeed love, nor are we able to prioritize the goods that we love. That last is a weakness from which Augustine regularly prays to be relieved, citing a famous text from the *Song of Songs*, at 2.4: 'Order my love in me'.

Our Augustine will want to distinguish his view of love not only from that of the pagans, but also from that of many post-Reformation Christians. Replying to twenty-first-century men and women, he will expound *his* position, not that attributed to him by Luther, Calvin or their more modern successors. Without going into detail, we should emphasize that Augustine never taught that mankind is totally corrupt as a result of the 'fall': rather that our innate capacity for love of God and the Good has been severely damaged, leaving us lame and limping and in need of support (PJ, 2.4). We suffer both from an 'ignorance' of God – so that our understanding of the difference between right and wrong is diminished – and from a lack of the will power necessary to resist our varying weaknesses and to do the right thing even if we want to and (more or less) know what ought to be done. We may perhaps have second-order desires for the right thing, though a second-order 'desire' and its first-order parallel are not the same kind of desire: in illustration Augustine will remind us of his sexual frailties as he recorded them in the *Confessions*: he did not want to be chaste but wanted to want to be chaste. But such second-order desires will also now be impaired!

Our love of goodness is thus regularly unable to achieve what it strives after. We are divided: we both want and do not want the right thing. Hence, either we fail to do it or we do it half-heartedly; or conversely we may regret not having the 'guts' to steal or fornicate when we have the chance. Now Augustine will draw attention to some non-theological facts. First, the general moral problem thus evoked had already been noted well before his time – and not only by philosophers, nor only by Christians. Plato in the *Republic* (4.439e) had famously alluded to a man who could not resist looking at corpses; Aristotle had examined the problem of weakness of will more exhaustively in book seven of the *Nicomachean Ethics*.

Ovid, who can scarcely be convicted of moral perfectionism, had noted how 'I know and approve the better but I follow the worse' (*Metamorphoses* 7.20-21).

Such writers had shown Augustine how to reflect on the phenomenon of the divided moral self well before he read Paul's letter to the Romans. Like the earlier poets and philosophers, he did not need to invoke specifically religious claims to see the problem. His remarks about the weakness of the will to goodness – or, as he would put it, the weakness of our love for what is good – depend (again) not on 'top-down' theological theory but empirical evidence. Of course, he strove to find a theological explanation of the data, but the data themselves do not derive from theology; knowledge of them is available to a more or less honest believer and a non-believer alike.

Yet though our wills and more basically our loves are divided, Augustine would reject the thesis that Luther and Calvin impute to him, that our 'erotic' power for good is entirely destroyed. We are not morally dead, as these Reformers preached, but we are badly enough mauled that we cannot stand on our two moral feet without divine assistance (however conveyed to us). We are able to injure ourselves – that theme will be examined in Chapter 3 – but we cannot cure ourselves (so T, 13.12.16). And psychologically, our Augustine will insist, his rejection of the Reformed account of moral inadequacy is of great importance. What he will be defending in our century is not *any* version of Christianity, but his own account of it; those who fail to provide evidence for their own perverse reading of him he will adjudge heretical.

For Augustine urges that without some trace of a proper self-love and self-respect – we cannot – unless we are to become someone else, or God – learn to love or respect others. Thus he will reject interpreting the recorded words of Jesus that 'You should love your neighbour as yourself', as do some of our latter-day Reformed – to mean 'You should love your neighbour in the future in the way that you loved yourself in the past': that is, that love of neighbour must *replace* love of self. Certainly if we were morally dead – which, as he emphasized, is not his position – we should be unable to have any non-selfish love of ourselves without or before the arrival of God's saving grace. But that, he will repeat, has never been his position: he does not confuse self-respect with selfishness, nor – in a secular version of his theory – would he *contrast* egoism with altruism. God does not do our moral work for us; he enables our restored selves to do it ourselves. Our Augustine is not on the side of overzealous do-gooders who unnecessarily burn themselves out. Arguments about the power (or even the need) for mankind to be possessed of an 'erotic' passion for God expose a deeper conflict among contemporary Christians. When our Augustine shall present himself as challenging contemporary ideas, he must clearly identify the version of Christianity he will assert to be authentic, and on which he is basing his challenge. Nor will he deny that in his interpretation of biblical accounts of love he often expresses himself in the language of Platonic philosophy.

And that, according to a second group of Reformers, was precisely what is wrong with him. For while one group of Reformers misinterpreted him, by others he has been seen as at best a compromiser, a fence-sitter who has blended Christianity with Greek philosophy, thus ceasing to be a strict sort – for some, any sort – of Christian. This is not the place for him to offer a detailed rebuttal of this now gradually receding yet still recurring canard. Sufficient for him to point out that the more serious and honest of those who profess a Reformed view have had to admit – paradoxically – as did Harnack, that a supposedly non-Christian Hellenism is already to be found in the New Testament, especially in the writings attributed to St John. If we are to judge the New Testament as theologically contaminated, how, Augustine will ask, are we to find an original prototype by which 'authentic' Christianity is to be assessed?

Whatever the answer, Augustine has now reached the third of his basic themes, and that in virtue of which he finds himself particularly unpopular among many in the twenty-first century, whether secularists or *soi-disant* Christians whose overriding concern appears as to remain in communion (it has been well put) with the *Guardian, Le Monde* or the *New York Times*. That third theme is the continuing and ineradicable reality of sin in human individuals and human society – though for the moment we can well drop that offensive word 'sin', smacking of unwanted theological explanation or even fantasy. Let Augustine, for the time being at least, be content with 'evil' or perhaps 'moral evil'; that should not be too much of an immediate burden for him. In fifth-century Hippo he kept puzzling over what is the origin of evil, whether moral or 'natural': examples of the latter being the fate of the victims of a tsunami or a volcanic eruption; of the former – and urgently pressing on Augustine himself – the frequent terrible sufferings of young children (AJ, 5.1.4; IW, 2.22).

First then the facts: Augustine lived in an age when evil was not difficult to be observed, even by the relatively privileged and free members of society. The Roman Empire – barbarous though it had always been in many respects, and not least in its increasingly savage penal system – had served one good purpose in reducing the chance of random death and destruction. Citizens of the Empire could travel with a much-reduced fear of thieves or murderers. For women (as in dangerous times also for men) there was less risk of being raped by marauding soldiers, or having your house burnt down. For Christians by Augustine's day there was no risk of finishing up in the amphitheatre at the wrong end of a lion if you were too visible a worshipper. Above all, you knew where you were: if you followed the rules, you could hope to survive. In a modern idiom: 'If everyone does what s/he is told, no one will get hurt!'

By the time of Augustine's death in a Hippo under siege by the Vandals and soon to be destroyed, all that was changing for the worse. The 'Roman peace' was yielding, even in the previously quiet backwaters of North Africa, to a menacing uncertainty: you might now be killed tomorrow, or tortured for wealth you did not possess, as were some bishops. Yet even in earlier more peaceful and orderly times – quite apart from man-made miseries – life was comparatively short: females would frequently die in childbirth, and plagues and sicknesses were rampant; Augustine himself, as we have noted, was particularly moved by the seemingly quite unwarranted suffering of young children. In view of all this, it is hardly surprising that he found this 'darkness of social life' (CG, 19.6) horrific – nor was there reason to expect that things would get any better; for most people the world was grim. Our Augustine will insist that his account of life in fifth-century Hippo as often nasty, brutish and short is not to be dismissed as gloomy pessimism, but accepted as clear-eyed honesty. He will say the same of conditions in much of our contemporary world.

When the first major intellectual crisis of Christianity as a whole hit Europe in the eighteenth century, much of the barbarity remained, and further afield things may have seemed as bad if not worse than ever. But there appeared to be light at the end of a tunnel, the darkness of which was by some identified with the Christian religion. Close attention to the Old Testament, as we have already observed, suggested God was trivial, parochial, genocidal, arbitrary: in short, immoral and irrational. Such a god could not possibly exist; therefore, as proper objects of reverence we should elevate Man and his Reason. No one seemed to explain why man was so reasonable, let alone that he was, in whole or in part, a fit object of worship. Yet even in the nineteenth century Mill – the self-confessed atheist from birth – still seemed at the end of his life to suppose that man could become so! Nor, Augustine will point out, should we assume that such attitudes have disappeared; those who want to be 'freed' from religion often seem – absurdly – to suppose that science shows them how such 'freedom' can be attained, perhaps in some 'trans-human' society.

Attempts to dissolve the apparent difficulties with such 'progressivist' claims were (and are) forthcoming: man had failed thus far because superstitious, lacking confidence, hence relying on the Christian God. According to Rousseau, Voltaire, Comte and many other avowed or implicit worshippers of the idealized and idolized self, the process of sweeping away Christianity and many social brutalities, such as torture, traditionally accompanying it, will soon be completed – torture persisted, it was pointed out, in the Papal States – and we shall be able to concentrate on education as the path not to a merely good life but to becoming godlike, inheriting God's supposed powers (in a voluntarist age) to make and remake the moral order. Some of this confidence, though surprisingly little, was shaken when after 1789 the abolition in France of God and king led not to peaceful progress but to the Jacobin Terror, in which characteristically not even the killers were safe but rational dog ate rational dog.

What our Augustine will remind us was forgotten or ignored is that education can bring a rationalizing arrogance as well as a cultural and intelligent richness to human life. Indeed, as theologian par excellence of older ways, he knows that he has increasingly been viewed as the *fons et origo* – no longer as the reporter – of European and Western darkness. As Comte saw it, the age of religion was giving way to the age of metaphysics, which in its turn will give way to the age of science. That new 'theology' that is sociology will prepare the way for the new paradise of scientism: we shall all be happy and Augustine can be consigned to the scrap-heap.

Our Augustine will retort that the deluded, self-satisfied cosiness of the Enlightenment dream should be (but is not) viewed as impossible in the present world. There may have been some excuse, he will continue, for his being presented as a doleful pessimist before the disasters on which the curtain rose in 1914, but none of those living since then have any excuse for persisting in their facile self-flattery. They have seen the Nazis, the Stalinists (not only in the Soviet Union), the Holocaust, the killing fields of Cambodia and Ruanda, the atrocities now proclaimed as holy by Muslim fanatics: and that just for starters. It is easy at times to get the impression that the human race is crazed, infected by some primal sin – exactly, Augustine will point out, what he always supposed it to be!

There is a sense in which the problem of evil exists only for monotheists who try to justify the ways of God to men. But if we did not have the Augustinian problem of evil, we should have what intelligent Greek predecessors of Augustine understood very well: no paradise but an 'age of iron' in which atrocity, enslavement and the rest of our self-inflicted misfortunes abound. Compared with that bleak alternative – so well displayed by the poet Sophocles whose *Oedipus the King* was considered by Aristotle the greatest of the tragedies, arguably as the best presentation of a world according to the basic hopes and fears of Greek culture – what Augustine offers was and is positively optimistic: the chance of heaven, if not on earth, then beyond it. Those of us who cannot be bothered with God or who think a moral world too demanding, Augustine invites to consider the alternative: arguably a more banal version of the 'fate' hanging over the Greeks. Misery persists for most people, though we the comfortable will look the other way for as long as we can, and some of the more thoughtful or sensitive among us will commit suicide in despair.

Augustine, as we shall see, will insist that the alternative to his Christian vision is (at least for the vast majority of us) savagery and death, with no redemption, the only escape being a facile optimism that must be entirely self-deluding: a mere whistling in the wind. A recent film about concentration camps is absurdly titled *La Vita è Bella* (Life Is Beautiful). Life in a concentration camp is not beautiful, though whether through heroism or a whistling in the wind a glimmer of goodness can from time to time be found even there. As Heraclitus said long ago about his doubtless stinking privy, 'Here too there are gods'. Only the blind, our Augustine will assert, will call him a pessimist about human society. Nor is there much reason to suppose that society will change substantially for the better, unless in a few fortunate enclaves and for limited periods of time.

Augustine developed earlier Christian accounts of human malevolence into his theory of original sin, preaching that *qua* members of the human race, we have all sinned in Adam. He will tell us, as he told the people of Hippo, that the data came first: his theory of our double life ('common' as linked descendants of Adam – perhaps now he might settle for daughters of mitochondrial Eve – and 'personal' from our individual conception till death) being an attempt (within a theistic framework) to make sense of it. He will add that human society is even worse than a dispassionate analysis would suggest, and despite many fine things many humans do. That is because there is a God who is good, and the atrocities we humans commit are not only crimes against ourselves (directly or indirectly) but crimes – now he will revert to the word 'sins' – against God in the person of Jesus Christ.

Yet our Augustine will tell us how, against this sombre background, the Christian vision shines out the more brightly: how in the twenty-first century he can find much more to say in support of original sin: a theory that he (as also his eighteenth-century opponents) knows very well draws strength from the observed malignity of much human behaviour, and while not making it intelligible, certainly makes it expectable and unsurprising. As Augustine tells it, such behaviour is unintelligible because irrational, because ultimately directed toward unrealistic goals like human omnipotence. When curiously unpleasant crimes are committed, our journalists regularly remark on them as inexplicable. By liberal standards it is certainly inexplicable, indeed inconceivable. Yet it happens, and Augustine will tell us why it is only to be expected in what he calls this 'darkness of social life'.

2

'Scientific' Philosophy and First-Person Confession

Scholars sometimes say, not entirely accurately but nonetheless informatively, that Plato thought individuality something to outgrow. Aristotle quite specifically says that philosophy cannot speak of the individual as such, since of the individual there is no definition (*Metaphysics* Z.1036a). Thus, when we construct a syllogism, we say, 'All men are mortal', then 'all Greeks are men', and conclude that therefore 'all Greeks are mortal'. Here, 'all Greeks' is a set, and we think of ourselves philosophically only as members of a set. Even if the minor premise reads, 'Socrates is a man', we still only comprehend him as a typical man.

In the writings of recent philosophers about the human individual we recognize two strong tendencies. One approach will emphasize the 'atomic' individual with subjective wishes and desires, even the desire to be self-constituting so far as this is possible, and even perhaps with the aid of genetic manipulation to make oneself into a 'trans-human' 'person', thus able to act as a kind of mini-creator, or mini-god. The other approach points in the opposite direction; it is supposedly more scientific and its supporters tend to see individuals as statistics, thus following Aristotle but going beyond his admission that we cannot philosophize about the individual as such, but only think of him as member of a set. For on this second view membership of a group is *all* that matters.

Most medieval philosophers followed Aristotle in asking why there is plurality of individuals in each set (why there are many men, cows, etc.), and claiming that the cause of the plurality is matter (or sometimes form). They rarely concerned themselves with the differences between individuals within the human set, not even with the subsets of males and females, normally contenting themselves with little more than the popular opinion (or with Aristotle's more sophisticated version) that females are incomplete males. This 'scientific' approach persists into our own times in more bizarre, indeed sinister, forms. Many contemporary thinkers have supposed that differences between individuals should be eliminated by assimilation of the individual to the State (the Third Reich in the case of Heidegger), or to the 'proletariat' (or to some supposedly discriminated-against subgroup among the 'proletariat') in the case of various Marxist or post-Marxist alternatives.

Or if not that political solution, then in order to show that philosophy *can* treat of individuals, we are urged to eliminate all 'first and second person' discourse from 'scientific' speech – thus recasting, say, 'I love you' as 'There is a loving and/or sexual relationship between person X and person Y' (or Spouse 1 and Spouse 2). Despite its seeming a bit strange if 'the "average Canadian" (as an economist ironically has put it) has one breast and one testicle', statistics (often recklessly advanced) can be taken to tell us all we need to know – all that is important – about ourselves as individuals. Hence we are often reduced, in effect, to economic or consumer cogs, or to totalitarian soldiers trained as killing machines: so long as we kill (or produce), that is all that is required of us; that is what we are for, and we are substitutable – more or less, though some may be less effective than others – until the supply runs out – which in a war means the other side winning. In such an impersonal world there can be no enduring moral or aesthetic values, no sense of individual responsibility, no distinction between actions and events – an action being merely the name of an event involving humans rather than, say, falling masonry.

Obviously philosophers like Aristotle or Thomas Aquinas who declined to talk philosophically about qualitatively distinguishable individuals (believing they can merely be *recognized* by the senses or the mind – I see you, and know that it is you, and similarly I can think about you) would have had no time for such 'scientific' descriptions of humanity. They are hardly to be blamed because their attempts to write scientifically have degenerated into 'scientism'. For there are many other factors involved in the modern desire to depersonalize the 'self' that it is not our business – nor Augustine's – to discuss here. Nevertheless, there is no doubt that past neglect of personal difference – especially surprising in the case of Christian thinkers who claimed that human beings are formed in some sort in God's image – at least opened the door to the contemporary mentality when the chance arose from what appeared a possible outcome of the successes of experimental science. Without science there is no scientism, and surprisingly enough one of those who in important respects followed Augustine's very different example (though he denied it) was among those scientists who pointed us towards scientism. Augustine gives way to Descartes.

Nor was Augustine the only exception, among major thinkers of the more distant past, to the mentality to which I allude. The ancient Stoics castigated Plato and Aristotle because, so they thought, they could have paid more philosophical attention to individual differences not only among living things but among every kind of set, even down to grains of sand. Plotinus worried that positing a Form of Man might not account for the particular identity of Socrates; there might need to be an individual Form of Socrates. In the fourteenth century, Duns Scotus thought that too many of his fellow Aristotelians neglected what he called the 'this-ness' (*haecceitas*) of things: for which he earned the praises of the poet Gerard Manley Hopkins. Compared with the boldness of Augustine, however, all these claims seem peripheral, almost trivial. The Stoics and Plotinus and Scotus (though not Hopkins) considered the problem simply as metaphysical; they held that metaphysics can and should be able to do what Aristotle said it could not.

Perhaps we are trying to run before we have learned to walk. We have noted that there is limited truth in Plato's holding individuality something to outgrow. There is, however, another very different feature of Platonism: in the empirical world (so Plato points out in the *Meno* and the *Theaetetus*), knowledge is distinguished from true opinion by being first-hand: we 'know' how to go from Athens to Larissa if we have travelled the road ourselves, not merely following what we learn from reading a map or from the directions of others. At a more 'metaphysical' level, our experience of Forms is also first-hand: I do not know the Form of the Good (though I may learn something about it) by reading a Platonic dialogue. I only know it when I 'see' and love it.

As we have noted, in metaphysics Augustine is a Platonist, as to a degree all reflective Christians must be; thus, thinking once more about Plato may help us understand something of why he declined to follow the full Platonic line on individuals. Plato apparently supposed, at least at times, firstly that we value people for the qualities they have – hence that there is no value to be discerned in the person as such – and then that personal differences, even as revealed in the virtues he so admired, represent inadequate efforts to reach a single perfection. If we were all morally and spiritually perfect – this he thought at times, but apparently not in the *Phaedrus* – we would be indistinguishable qualitatively, though not of course quantitatively. There would be no value in unique personal existence and no relation between quantitative differences and varieties of excellence. Yet it seems we cannot rank human excellences in any league-table order, just as we cannot rank many of the greatest works of art, splendid as they all are – though perhaps Plato can claim that they are measurable by God with reference to the 'exemplar laid up in heaven'.

Be that as it may, in his judgements about the ideal human being Plato failed to recognize that the spatio-temporal situation of each of us will affect the nature of our possible excellences (or lack of them). He relies too often on our being able to establish a ranking of excellences apart from the unique context – with its unique opportunities – of the life of each individual. Although he could not know, as we do, that a physical aspect of each individual – his or her genetic code – is distinct and irreplaceable, he *was* in a position to know that, if not genetically, at least historically, every individual is different from every other; hence that every individual has different opportunities and therefore necessarily differing modes of living the good life.

Plato seems to accept the characteristic Greek attitude that differences always indicate superiority and inferiority, as strikingly in the case of the difference between males and females (in which regard he was far less adrift than most). There is no reason to suppose that Augustine would persist with that error in the third millennium since even in the fifth century he was able to recognize that with reference to love, the root of all the virtues, women (He instances Mary Magdalene) were frequently superior to men. In the twenty-first century he would be able to provide substantiation to the view of the complementarity of the sexes.

Arrived in the twenty-first century, moreover, our Augustine will criticize our attitudes to human individuals on at least two important counts. He will observe that between the end of antiquity and the late nineteenth century, Christians have devoted little serious thought to the thesis, so prominent in his own day, that human beings are created in God's image. He will not claim, he continues, that they dismissed it or denied it, or did not mention it frequently enough. Yet they added little to what they found in the Fathers (like himself) and took few occasions to develop the doctrine's implications, especially for moral and political philosophy and theology. Augustine's second complaint will be more general and more personal: that, as often happens with unconventional thinkers, some of his own most original ideas – in this case about individuals – were paid little more than lip service, were misinterpreted or largely forgotten.

As we have already emphasized, Augustine's philosophical originality was fostered by an unusual intellectual history very different from that of most of his more learned Christian contemporaries. We need to remember that when we turn to our immediate subject: his approach to the problem of unique human individuals and his claim that to understand individuals and individual excellences it is not enough just to think of them metaphysically as members of the human race. A different approach must be developed: to attend – as Plato did not – to their historical situations in place and time, and thus to the possibilities and impossibilities for excellence available to each of them.

Augustine's specifically Latin culture brought two advantages, one positive, the other negative: the negative was that he did not have to follow the broad approach of Greek-speaking Christian Platonism established by Origen in the third century and gradually corrected before and after Augustine's time. Augustine's *Platonism* is derived primarily from readings in the philosophy of Plotinus as translated by that earlier Latin-speaking orator and convert to Christianity, Marius Victorinus. Coming from a different culture from contemporary Greek bishops and a Christian culture as yet less standardized intellectually, Augustine could give free rein – here is the positive advantage – to his own talents, and his self-confidence in the handling of his sources. He could think philosophically within his own world while over time gradually gaining an adequate grasp of what the Greeks were up to: this he acquired from Ambrose, the learned bishop of Milan who baptized him, and from his friend, and Ambrose's episcopal successor, Simplicianus (who asked him some very hard questions of biblical exegesis), and from many others. Nevertheless, his basic culture was Latin, Cicero his earliest and most consistent intellectual teacher.

And as we have already noticed, one of the many benefits the young Augustine received from Cicero was to be introduced to the debate – still being pursued in Cicero's lifetime after 200 years – between the Stoics and a group of the Sceptics. These latter – the so-called Academics – had long taken over Plato's Academy and argued that scepticism was the basic philosophy of both Plato himself and of his master Socrates. The principal dispute between Stoics and Sceptics concerned the possibility of knowledge, as distinct from justified or plausible belief, but although, as we have seen, Augustine remained sceptical of the possibility of much strictly philosophical 'knowledge', he felt no more difficulty than Descartes in accepting the certain knowledge that he exists.

Augustine discusses knowledge of his own existence several times, but the example most often cited in succeeding centuries (with good reason) is the following (CG, 11.26; T, 15.12.21): 'I am (aware that I am) mistaken, therefore I exist'. What is important about this is not only the self-referential nature of the argument – 'I can only deny that I exist if I exist' – but the emphasis placed on the 'I'. Augustine thinks it informative *about the world* to refer to himself as 'I', even while he readily admits that he has little understanding of his own nature. He is aware that in the twenty-first century some want to 'dissolve' the self, but replies that such objections misconstrue his account of self-knowledge: his is a dynamic, not an inert self – and that is sufficient to deconstruct radical objections to 'self-hood' as irredeemably reductionist.

Augustine's present concern is less with the form of his argument than with placing at the centre of his thought that 'I', that is, the 'non-scientific' first person and its relationship with the 'you' of the second person: first with the 'you' of the second person which is God, then with human second persons who are properly to be viewed 'in God'. God and other persons are not mere things, and for Augustine our relationship with them and awareness of our relationship with them are facts of philosophical life. As he has already pointed out, he makes no claim to understand, let alone 'capture' the 'I'; he only holds that there *is* an 'I' and that that 'I' and its unique individuality, created by God and only intelligible with reference to God, are of a literally vital importance.

If metaphysics cannot explain the 'I' (which it cannot if it deals with human beings only as members of a set), Augustine must find some other mode of enquiry to assist him: then he will have more chance of at least some success. The mode of enquiry he settles on, especially in *The City of God*, is in cultural terms historical, while at the level of the individual *qua* individual it is biographical or autobiographical. Writing in that mode in the *Confessions* he assumes that to talk intelligibly *about* God and himself must be simultaneously to pray to God in thanksgiving for being what one is.

Whether Augustine consciously intended to supplement metaphysics with history and retrospective autobiography is uncertain. The persistence of such an approach from the time of the *Soliloquies*, then more strikingly in the *Confessions* – finally in his much later analysis of culture in *The City of God* – is a strong argument that we should suppose that he did, his original intuition perhaps eventually giving place to an explicit recognition of this needing to be done. At very least we must conclude that he gradually became more aware of the relevance of historical and biographical enquiry, while with such growing awareness he became more and more specifically Christian and – formally at least – less fully devoted to Platonism in its contemporary 'pagan' understanding.

As we have seen, and like most other ancient thinkers, Platonists paid less than adequate attention to the differences between individuals within the human species. By contrast, it became the more pressing for Augustine to think not only about Augustine the man, but about Augustine the particular man in his uniquely personal and particular set of circumstances. With his belief that man is created in the image of a personal God to support him, he can add to his Platonist metaphysic the individual and informative experiences of his providentially guided life – and those of the lives of others

Augustine well knew that success in this project requires humility, understood as a detailed awareness of his dependency as created and of his fallibility as fallen, especially since in the *Confessions* he sets out to explore how he was pulled by God in a specific direction, that is, towards baptism. In the *Unfinished Work against Julian* (1.110), and elsewhere, he cites, 'No-one comes to me unless the Father has drawn him' (*John* 6:44), and in the *Confessions* he reveals that he was drawn to God through the individual experiences of his unique life – often against his personal inclinations. Explaining his project to our 'scientific' metaphysicians, he will claim from his new and personalist approach to be able to understand more about his own nature, and *hence* about the complexities of human nature in general, than they could have achieved through their necessarily reductionist metaphysic alone. For though they assert, with Aristotle, that we can approach particulars through the senses and the mind, Augustine will add that by use of a literary form that he has almost invented, he can be successful in the understanding of individual human beings where 'scientific' or would-be scientific metaphysicians must fail. And what can be achieved for the individual in biography and autobiography can be done for individual cultures through historical and other literary evocations.

That Augustine can claim to have *'almost* invented' spiritual autobiography needs explanation; for there were other writings circulating in the ancient world – typically pagan and Christian – which seem at least precursors of Augustine's masterpiece. The first type – and perhaps in the twenty-first century Augustine might find this slightly embarrassing – is best represented by a work of Apuleius, a fellow North African whose 'Platonic' philosophical writings Augustine knew – and disliked – as he tells us in *The City of God*; and had he read the work to which I now allude – *The Golden Ass* (the American slang usage of 'ass' might seem not inappropriate to some of the content) – he would have liked it even less than its author's more philosophical ramblings. Surprisingly, however, this 'picaresque novel', cast in the first person, is in its way religious, describing the troubles brought on the hero – including his being transformed into the 'obscene' animal of its title – when he dabbles in sex and magic, and his eventual redemption as a devotee of the goddess Isis: a favourite deity allegorizable by Apuleius and others who thought of themselves as Platonists.

That *The Golden Ass* is in the first person and culminates in a conversion are not its only parallels with Augustine's *Confessions*. The sin of dabbling in magic of which the hero is guilty is precisely *curiositas*, or wanting to know what it is wrong to want to know or to seek to know. It is a 'favourite' sin of Augustine's, and along with the lust of the flesh and the desire to dominate forms his 'triple concupiscence'. Augustine and Apuleius are right: there are facts which we ought not want to know (however 'scientifically' interesting they may be). An unfortunately modern example would be how people react under novel forms of torture.

The Golden Ass differs from the *Confessions* in many ways, not least in that there is little doubt that Apuleius's motivations in writing it were less than entirely straightforward. It is a story that enables him to present all sorts of titillating information and adventure from low-life and having 'tabloid' appeal – and in the world of our modern tabloids a mix of religious and pornographic material is far from unknown, both helping to sell the paper or the book. *The Golden Ass*, as well as being religious, is picaresque, its hero, Lucius, being something of a Tom Jones. However, just as picaresque novels were popular among pagans in Imperial Roman times, so the growing Christian population found that it needed Christian and (ultimately) more edifying tales of sex and violence: these came in the form of stories, legendary or other, of Christian martyrs – preferably virgins.

We thus have two varieties of ancient 'chick-lit'. In the pagan version the hero manages to fornicate his way through many adventures until in the end he wins the love of his bride whose necessary virginity has been excitingly at risk throughout the story. In the Christian version the heroine, after surviving all sorts of 'pagan' attempts to deflower her, will finish up as a virgin martyr: so the reader gets the sexual excitement crowned with the edifying last scene. Augustine's *Confessions*, though far better written and intellectually superior to this kind of material, could and does appeal to the same mixture of motives in the minds of much more respectable readers.

Nevertheless, with the partial exception of Boethius's *Consolation of Philosophy*, Abelard's story of his personal misfortunes and Descartes's formally 'philosophical' attempt to discredit the claims of scepticism – nor should Dante's *Divina Commedia* pass unnoticed – philosophical writing in first-person mode had little impact for centuries either on Christian philosophers or Christians more generally. Someone who did recognize what it could do and tried both to imitate and at the same time to subvert Augustine was the anti-Christian Rousseau, writing in that eighteenth century when the dechristianization of Europe began in earnest. Rousseau, Augustine will have to admit, well understood the 'cosmic' and Augustinian importance of confessing, of speaking in the first person about the experiences of one's unique life as a member of the human race.

For Rousseau, of course, 'confessing' meant something very different. While Augustine lit on the form of autobiographical writing to bare his sinful self to God and to ask for mercy and further divine assistance, Rousseau uses the same form to do effectively the opposite: to make excuses for appallingly selfish and malicious behaviour, to claim that none of it was really his fault: that he was just trying to be 'authentic' and had been overwhelmed by the corrupt society in which he was obliged to live: 'it's not my fault, Gov.; I am sincere; it really is someone else's – anyone else's – fault rather than mine; perhaps it's your fault, Gov., for making me fallible'. That response fails, however, in implying that I have the capacity to recognize what it means to be fallible, but that I have no responsibility for what I have done and effectively *cannot* repent.

Nevertheless, in comparing the two *Confessions*, we recognize how, confronted with the modern world, our Augustine will have no time for the idea that being sincere (even in good faith, which he would think impossible) is anywhere near morally adequate. Which brings him by a devious route to three insights he will analyse to explain the kind of understanding autobiographical reflection on one's own circumstances will bring – and why without such reflection any account of the world will be radically inaccurate since blindly impersonal and thus reductionist.

As we have seen, Augustine's first insight relates to the essentially Christian virtue of humility. The second will see him demonstrate how honest appraisal of his own circumstances shows that different, if parallel, movements of the soul are perceptible in the lives of his friends. They too are on a pilgrim's journey parallel to his own, yet uniquely distinct. The third insight will reveal how 'God', as he expresses it, pulls him from one psychological 'place' to another: a pressure which can only be interpreted by way of retrospective autobiography or personal history. Of course, his move from place to place is brute fact: the theological explanation presents God's activity as the only possible explanation of it. Thus again Augustine offers empirical data to be explained as theology, as he invites us to investigate each in turn of his insights about the journey of his life and self-discovery.

Augustine had known Christianity before he came to Italy and finally decided to be baptized by Ambrose in Milan, but in a form intellectually unacceptable in that it took both God and the soul to be material substances. Now, both from his reconstructed understanding of Christianity and from those Platonist readings that helped inspire that reconstruction, he recognizes an immaterial soul, an immaterial first principle of the universe and man as a necessarily dependent being.

From his Christian instructors Augustine learned that the universe and all mankind were created from nothing by God but that, for whatever reason, we humans forget that fact as inconvenient. At the same time he read something comparable in Plotinus (*Ennead* 5.1.1), namely that we have forgotten our 'father' and hence our selves. Though we derive from the activity of a superior being, we pretend, want to pretend and enjoy pretending, that we are self-creators. That dream our Augustine will now tell us is similar to those of some postmodern thinkers – as also of many liberal-minded opinion-formers and judges – who, though admitting that we have not *yet* established ourselves as self-creators, hope we can, or even must, eventually attain to that condition. Our Augustine, still not impressed, points to the passage in his *Confessions* (2.4.9; 2.6.12; 2.6.14) about stealing pears when he was a teenager: that sort of thing we do 'wilfully': that is, solely because we want to do it and ultimately to delude ourselves that we are or can be – morally at least – self-creators: thus from mere pride we indulge in apostasy from God. And he will cite *Ecclesiasticus* 10:9ff: 'The beginning of sin is pride', together with the Plotinian parallel.

That brings Augustine back to that first insight which tells us that we can recognize our nature as individual members of the human species. We must be humble, and that humility implies two different recognitions. First, as we have indicated, our well-being depends ultimately on God, but also – as Augustine gradually came to learn – on the special attitude ('in the Lord') to other people. Secondly, as well as recognizing our dependence, we must recognize that we are unavoidably prone to evil behaviour: we are victims, in Augustine's gradually developing theological explanation of that and other phenomena, of 'original sin'. Our requisite humility, however, is not to be confused with servility or abjectness or what Aristotle (*Nicomachean Ethics* 3 1125a33) thought a refusal to admit what is good about ourselves as well as what is bad; and which would constitute a rejection of truth. On the contrary, Augustine teaches that humility is precisely the recognition of a *fact*: that we are – in theological language – dependent sinners.

In his *Confessions* Augustine has a good deal to say about the different temptations and perverse desires that impeded his own moral progress and that of his friends, especially Alypius. In his own case the problem was sex, and Africans had a reputation for lust, though by the standards of his times when any slave-owner had access to the bodies of his slaves, male or female, he might seem comparatively restrained. Nevertheless, he believed himself incapable of giving up sexual activity, and when his long-time girlfriend was sent back from Milan to Africa so that he could make the kind of marriage that would help him in his career, he had to have a new woman in the meantime.

With Alypius things were different; for him the impulse was not sex but violence, in particular the ritualized slaughter at gladiatorial shows in the amphitheatre; these even Christian rulers as yet felt little inclination to stop, presumably since there were too many *aficionados* like the 'blood-crazed' Alypius. Augustine writes of Alypius to point to the different 'lusts', actual or potential, in different people; if God is to help us overcome them he has to fit the remedy to the individual case, as in Augustine's view he has done – at least for his elect.

Shortly before writing his *Confessions*, Augustine faced a crisis in his intellectual life, which he afterwards remembered and clearly recognized. It was brought about by a request from Simplicianus, his old Neoplatonizing mentor in Milan, now become bishop. Recognizing Augustine's intellectual capacity, Simplicianus sent him a number of knotty points to resolve in interpretation of the Scriptures, especially in Paul's letter to the Romans. In trying to resolve Simplicianus's difficulties, Augustine made what he took to be a divinely inspired theological discovery, which he would find overturned his understanding of the relationship between God and man and of man's ability to act as he should. For he now determined that the correct interpretation of texts like 'What do you have which you have not received?' (I *Corinthians* 4:7) indicates the beginnings of faith as a special gift of God and to be received as such.

The long-term implications of Augustine's new theology for moral philosophy will be treated in the next chapter. Now he believes not that God automatically rewards those he foresees will seek him, but that the very ability to seek him is divinely given. Acquisition of faith is beyond a man's natural powers, which are insufficient to bring human desire for good to its necessary fulfilment even in ordinary moral behaviour, let alone in faith in God. Rather, as we have seen, man will try, insofar as he can, to make a god of himself, and the possibility of that may vary, or seem to vary, with the development of those 'Promethean' capacities exalted among the early post-Christian and neo-pagan Romantics. At *Confessions*

8.7.17, our Augustine will remind us, he gives an example of the sort of truth he discovered about the possibility of moral action (at least in hard cases): he found himself praying, 'Give me chastity, but not yet!' In the words of the Roman poet, he knew the better and did the worse – nor did he in any real time soon want to do the better.

God is the giver even of faith in himself: the gift is entirely gratuitous and in no way deserved, nor – in more modern language – has anyone a right to it, for in a naturalistic world there can be no rights, certainly not against a god. The true God, however, tailors his gifts to the state and weaknesses of the individual recipients: as we have seen, the weakness of Augustine was for sex, of Alypius for violence. For others it might be for booze; there are many possibilities. In each case we can injure but cannot cure ourselves without God's aid.

In the ancient world when philosophers thought about the difficulties confronting those who wished for 'happiness', however described, and for the 'good life', they regularly recognized two enemies in their path: these they would broadly identify as pleasure and pain. You can be seduced or terrified, and either way you will lose your moral compass. Then, Augustine tells us, you will start to rationalize a decision to forget about morality, perhaps constructing metaphysical, quasi-metaphysical or anti-metaphysical belief-systems to justify your choice of direction.

Religious thinkers habitually suppose that God will avail himself of either or both of these two sorts of pressure – that is, of pleasure and pain; so the fear of the Lord is the beginning of wisdom – and they may envisage that fear in unpleasantly hellish terms. But our business now is not with how God terrifies but with how he 'seduces': how he leads by that pleasure which is, Augustine believes, part of a loving 'weight' on the soul drawing us to good or – when selflessness is denied – to evil. We do things in the hope that we shall enjoy doing them, at least in the longer run.

Pleasure (as most philosophers in the ancient world agree) should not be pursued as an end; rather it should be welcomed as an accompaniment of right choices and actions – and the better you are, the more pleasure right action will give you. There is no reason to reject pleasure as morally irrelevant or necessarily misleading – pace the Kantians. It can and should help us do what is right and for the right reasons. That, for Augustine, is God's view of it, who continues to motivate us as the unique individuals he has created, drawing us slowly but surely, appropriately and satisfyingly. In his first lengthy treatment of the theme (RS 1.2.21-22) he uses the word *congruenter* to indicate the nature of this appropriate satisfaction, and in the *Confessions* he explains it from his own experience. When we do the right thing – as it were being pushed by God, and often against our apparent will – we derive increasing satisfaction from what we do. Pleasure, as the Platonists and others taught Augustine, takes its moral and spiritual character from its objects, that is, from the moral and spiritual status of what we love.

Here then is the 'new theology' of Augustine's response to Simplicianus about what Paul tells the Romans in his letter, and Augustine in the *Confessions* applies it to his own life thus far. He is not concerned to get every detail right, all 'in one go' – sometimes he may appear to fall short in that regard – but rather by hindsight, by historical reflection, to grasp the general trajectory of the passing years. He has travelled a long way: from his rejection of the 'materialist' Christianity of North Africa, via the materialist dualism of the religion of Mani, through a period in which he eventually determined that radical scepticism is an irrational option, to his final decision to be received as a Catholic Christian in a baptismal pool still visible below street level in Milan.

As he was travelling, of course, he did not realize where he would finish up, but eventually, in Newman's words – and in the experience of many of us – he found himself in another place. But it was still himself he found there, and it is himself that he remembers; he would have been staggered – even frightened – if he seriously believed (rather than merely claimed) he was someone else. That he had made that journey was indisputable, and the explanation of it became the theological schema he worked out in his reply to Simplicianus. For, as we have already noticed, Augustine proceeds by looking at his personal history, as that of others, indeed at the unique history on a larger scale of his own culture – a particular group of people in a particular time and place who can be observed historically – then finds a theological explanation for what he observes. The whole is seen to make sense as a journey, and as intelligible, so not a matter of mere chance. It is this that makes a theological account a possibility: Augustine challenges us to offer a better explanation, for he now agrees with Dostoyevski that intelligibility in itself demands an explanation, indeed that it points to God.

And the explanation sought, Augustine now knows, will be both historical and metaphysical: metaphysical in that it depends on certain basic beliefs about human nature – as that it is fallen and that we are capable of envisaging a world better than that in which we normally live: a world dreamed of in anticipation by Plato and confirmed by Revelation. It offers a value system – Plato's moral Forms becoming divine attributes – not of our making, but governing our destinies and making them intelligible, and such that its non-existence would render such intelligibility impossible. The historical aspects of the vision involve us in individual thoughts, individual plans, individual successes and failures, not on such truths about the human race as a whole as that we are mortal, that each of us is born and after a short period of time dies.

We must reflect on our personal destiny, on where we go or where we are led, and in doing so we may begin to understand ourselves as individual members of our species. Yet Augustine himself has said and not least in the *Confessions* – see especially 10.8.12 ff. on memory – that we do *not* understand ourselves and our own internal dynamism: that we are a great mystery to ourselves, such that we do not *know* morally at least how we shall behave tomorrow, indeed whether we shall be alive tomorrow. Preaching in Hippo in 411, he told his congregation:

I, the bishop who speak to you in the name of the Lord, do not know what kind of man I am, and how much less do you know. I can have some notion of what I am at this moment, but how can I know what I shall be and when I shall become it. (S, 340A)

Writing like that, what was (and is) Augustine trying to tell us? Would he view the answers to that challenge in the same way now as once in Hippo? To answer those questions we need to look at his thoughts on time and on the soul: the former he would hardly wish to change, but about the soul he changed his mind significantly, and largely about the relationship between the soul and the body.

First, and briefly: time is a theme he treats both in the *Confessions* and in *On the Trinity*, noting that he knows what time is, 'but if I am asked what it is and would like to explain it, I do not know how to' (C, 11.14.17). For though time is an objective reality as created by God, it is envisaged by us by a 'distension' of the mind. Being possessed of *immaterial* souls, we are able not only to retain some contact with occurrences known in the past, but to transcend the material and restore that past to some new and present existence. To a degree too we can also predict the future; and, through 're-viewing' our past experiences, intuit ourselves as dynamic, and not – as Hume's critique of Descartes assumed – inert and static 'selves'. No 'material' soul – as of an animal dependent solely on bodily senses – can achieve anything like this.

In his earlier career as a Christian thinker, Augustine supposed that *we* are to be identified with our souls – generating problems about the soul's relationship with the body that he attempted to solve by claiming that in our present and passing life *we* use our bodies like tools to perform our daily tasks. That is a Platonic-sounding theory – whether and in what sense, if any, Plato would have accepted it is not our present concern. As a Christian, Augustine could not be satisfied with it for long, since it implies not only a denial of the resurrection of the body, but the jettisoning of the entire theology of the Incarnation and the physical birth of Jesus as a man. Thus the religious objections, but Augustine was also concerned about more philosophical problems, and these left him in a strange situation. Eventually (in *The Soul's Nature and Origin* 4.2.3) he would castigate those (including his earlier self) who held that 'we' are just our souls and can understand ourselves without reference to the body. Yet he has no philosophical tools to explain the 'mixture' of soul and body which as 'persons' – and he introduces the term for that 'mixture' (L, 137.3.11) – we must be.

Nevertheless, it is certain that in the twenty-first century he will not accept the theory proposed by Descartes – one of the founders of modern and postmodern thought and a man in some respects his apostate disciple – of what 'I' am. For Descartes subscribed to something at first sight close to the view that 'I' am my soul, arguing that the real 'I' is an immaterial substance, though of a significantly different sort from that advocated by the early Augustine, let alone by Plato. The Cartesian 'I', or *ego*, is strictly and solely a *rational* substance; of itself it is devoid of desires and apparently inert, which neither the Platonic nor the Augustinian soul could be. So Descartes is left with a problem superficially similar to but substantially different from that facing Augustine – and that is to say nothing of the science-fiction account he gives of a *tertium quid* by which he attempts to explain the very soul-body 'mixture' which Augustine admits he cannot comprehend.

Whereas Descartes supposed that we can recognize our 'self' by introspection, Augustine knows better; while to Hume's challenge that when he looks within himself he can find no substance but merely a bundle of activities – thoughts, desires, memories and so on – Descartes (unlike Augustine) has no reply, for what could an inert place-holder actually be? Whereas Descartes thought he could 'capture' the soul and identify the 'I' as a substantial self, Augustine not only could not explain the soul's relationship with the body but made no claim to comprehend its immaterial nature: immaterial not least, as we have seen, in that it can recall the past and to a degree predict the future. Yet since Augustine's soul is always functioning and never inert, it does not fall victim to Hume's critique. History can tell Augustine quite a lot about what he has been and become; what he actually is remains a mystery known only to God, as God himself is a mystery.

Augustine denies that we can discover our true nature by introspection, by inspecting our ever-changing selves and trying to 'fix' them, even to describe them. And worse, from the moral point of view, we are always liable to give ourselves the benefit of the doubt, to assert that our motives, for example, are pure, when we cannot know that they are and when we may have reason to suppose that they are not – even when we do 'the right thing'. 'Call no man just but God alone': in our present world there is no just man (nor, as we shall see, just war), but some people are more just – that is, less unjust – than others (and some wars are more just, that is, less unjust, than others, and thus perhaps necessary). To these we shall return in Chapter 4.

We could only know that our motives are pure – and thus what we are truly like – if we could act in wholly coherent fashion over a long period; thus theoretically at least Augustine agrees with the Stoics – from whom he probably learned – that a man could be wise for years without realizing it, and only retrospective autobiography could reveal it to him. But no retrospective autobiography can provide an account of our own nature with a detailed accuracy. Our nature as continuing individuals within the parameters of our species, Man – that is, in Augustinian language, our human soul – is constantly changing and cannot even in principle be 'captured' in the way it could be were it constituted on the Cartesian model.

Augustine thinks that we are creatures of habit, good or bad, and that our habits derive from repetitious acts in accordance with the pursuit of what we love and our avoidance of (or hostility to) what we hate. Yet there always remains a fluidity in our characters; that is why Augustine goes out of his way time after time to point to behaviour entirely out of keeping with the habits that our loves and hates have painfully and slowly built up. Notoriously (AJ, 3.11.22), he cites the case of a 'late-blooming' ascetic who had lived continently with his wife for more than twenty years but then bought a lyre-girl for sex. The mere fact that such bizarre and unpredictable behaviour can occur is evidence not only that we exist but that we are never, in this life, wholly determined. However good we are, we need to pray that we will stay that way; however bad we are, we still have the possibility of radical improvement. Replying to Simplicianus (1.2.22), Augustine told the ageing bishop that if he were to predict who would be saved and who would not, 'God would laugh at me'.

Augustine is already very unusual among philosophers in wanting to reflect on more than what can be said about men as a group within space and time, yet his way of describing the soul – in Descartes's language the 'self' – is also very different from that of his seventeenth-century successor. We have not yet uncovered the extent of that difference, but Augustine's concerns are altogether broader and less strictly epistemological.

To investigate them further we return to 'I am deceived, therefore I am' (CG, 11.26; T, 15.12.21), in which and similar arguments Augustine's immediate aim was limited to showing that he has beliefs about certain mental activities and that – whether those beliefs are true or false – they could not occur unless he exists. But what happens next? In the case of the seemingly parallel arguments of Descartes, we move from a certainty about my own existence to a similar certainty about the existence of God, thus ultimately to propositions about non-incorporeal items. Augustine moves differently, advancing, yes, from the existence of our minds to the existence of God; however, certainty is not his aim. Rather he wants to indicate, against both Manichaeans and more 'primitive' Christians, that God too must be a non-material substance. Even so, and as we have seen, he thinks attempts to find certainty philosophically to be normally misguided.

Contrary to Cartesian interpretations of his thought frequently offered in our own times (as for example by Charles Taylor in *The Sources of the Self*), behind Augustine's stance there lurks no problem of subjectivism; no one could reasonably object that he is trying to infer the nature of the external world from a subjectivist view of it. Like Plato, Aristotle, Epicurus and the Stoics, he takes the existence of the external world for granted, offering comment on it in terms of God's creative activity and of Platonic forms as divine attributes – in the case of ideas of creatable things, as concepts – in God's mind.

In contrast to the dramatic epistemological project of Descartes – his successors understood it as converting the central problems of metaphysics into epistemology (rather as he and they converted geometry into the more 'abstract' algebra) – Augustine wants to use arguments about his own existence to provide himself a place to stand when faced with what he ought to do and how he ought to live. When he looks within himself, what he dependently finds is only that he is godlike, God being more interior to him than he is to himself (C, 3.6.11). For Truth – that is God – lives in the 'inner man' (TR, 39.72), inasmuch as we have godlike capacities in a soul that can function as it does because it is immaterial.

Reflection on the fact that we can know that we exist but cannot know what we are – although we 'know' something of what we are – reveals one of the advantages of Augustine's view that our experience of life and our attempts to express it cannot be reduced to 'scientific' third-person language. Augustine makes no claim to understand the world only as we can construct it, let alone that all there is in the world is what we can construct: his concern with the first person, with what I do uniquely, enables him to conclude that scientific statements about the world have little importance for the individual asking the old Socratic question about how to live as well as possible – except that they provide the parameters within which, as a human being, I must develop my own behaviour.

I really do need to know that I am not a god, that *qua* human I have certain strengths and weaknesses, before I can determine what in my unique but restricted lifetime I can hope to do and do well. The basic weakness of what our Augustine will now dub the 'scientistic' alternative to his own position – a world view based on a scientistic ideology and a set of scientific facts supposedly able to eliminate the possibility of metaphysics – is that it will obscure all that is morally and spiritually important in human life. That, Augustine believes, is clear to everyone except those philosophers who want to think differently in their professional capacity from the way they cannot escape thinking in their ordinary lives.

None of that implies that Augustine will have to commit himself to denying the validity of, for example, what we might call 'pure research'. Rather it says that, if we were not individuals, pure research would have no intrinsic interest or importance; thus the areas of human experience with which scientific third-person research must concern itself (and with this Socrates would have agreed) can provide only a propaedeutic programme for living a life that matters, a fully human life. Obviously if, as many now say, nothing or virtually nothing matters, then Augustine is wholly mistaken. Yet without self-contradiction it is impossible to argue – as some have tried so to argue – that nothing matters (for even in a world in which – allegedly – nothing matters, one cannot escape enjoying or disliking things, thus attributing a certain importance to them). In any case, it does matter, our Augustine will observe, whether God exists or not: not least in that any answer to that question cannot but affect the lifestyles both of those who conclude that he exists and of those who deny it or want to deny it.

And our Augustine will go further. Some sort of understanding of the ever-changing self as it struggles on its way through life must be my ultimate concern if I am to construct my existence rationally, for why should I be more concerned with what happens 'out there', and has no impact on my own life, than with what has immediate and intimate impact? Again, his very word, 'intimate', Augustine will continue, points to God as the only possible explanation of my 'self' as an intelligible being. Only against a background of such intimacy can all sorts of non-propositional knowledge and experience enrich my life and increase my understanding of it: the experience of good literature, of listening to good music, of looking at great art and sculpture....

For it is hard to deny that we are both enriched by such experiences and learn something from them, and perhaps even harder to describe (in third-person terms) what precisely we have learned by watching *Hamlet*, listening to the *Archduke* or gazing almost in disbelief at Leonardo's *Last Supper*. No doubt everyone who has those experiences can say *something*, explain *something* that he or she has learned from them, but having made a few comments he may say to himself (or listen to someone else saying), 'Can that be all there is to it?' That response is analogous to his likely reaction if, being asked to describe a good friend, he mentions a few of his friend's characteristics – then realizes that no summary of qualities listed in a set of propositions is going to exhaust what it is to have this particular individual as a friend.

Augustine concludes that the intrinsic value of art is plausible only if we recognize self-discovery as more than identifying ourselves as members of the human race, or as significant in the scheme of things only insofar as members of the German *Volk*, the Marxist proletariat, the Fabian society, the gay lobbies or any other supposedly élite group, membership in which is from time to time deemed essential for those in tune with the March of History. Augustine's idea of the March of History is of a wholly different order and not invented by Man, scientistic or other.

3

Against Autonomy: 'Ought' and 'Can'

In philosophical debate through the centuries we can identify two rival accounts of 'freedom'. By the first, to be free is to be able to choose only the good, and that ability is not measured in terms of power or physical strength but of moral character. Few hold this position now, but it was dominant in antiquity and the Middle Ages. Thus, if I am in a position to shoot dead someone I dislike and to know that I can get away with it, but I reject the opportunity to do so, my decision is taken not because I lack the skill to take aim or the strength to pull the trigger, but because I have no will to act in that way; I am not that sort of person. If I do in fact open fire, I have let my feelings of anger master me; far from free, I am slave to a vicious passion. If I shoot because I am afraid that those urging me to do so may avenge themselves on me for not doing so, I am the slave of fear, another vicious passion. Of course, I can rationalize my behaviour, pretend that it is not my fault, but that does not change the viciousness of my act, nor that I am to blame for it (even though there may be extenuating circumstances depending on what I am afraid of); hard cases apart, however, the rationalizing would make me the more blameworthy. The very fact that I feel the need to rationalize indicates that I know that I did not have to act as I did; that is, I have not acted freely. Augustine's account of the true nature of freedom is along those lines; what we must long for – and hope to acquire in heaven – is the 'desired necessity' of being unable even to harbour thought of wrongdoing (IW, 5.61).

That is not how most of our contemporaries think of freedom; for them, especially but not only if they are existentialists, or if they fall, tacitly or otherwise, into some variety of postmodernism, to be free is to be able to choose without effective hindrance between alternative possibilities. Choice – normally exercised in view of immediate utility – is king, despite at least two sorts of strange moral consequence that seem to arise from its assumption, and not only for theists like Augustine but for anyone. For the theist it must seem absurd that God would (or being eternally present, could) do the right thing after weighing matters up and eventually deciding that he should act one way rather than another – perhaps perform a constructive rather than a destructive act. If we suppose him so 'choosing', our view of him is odd, indeed primitive.

Then God apart, and in the human context, it will also seem strange to suppose that in most instances – again I leave hard cases aside – one deliberates before deciding not to beat an innocent person rather than not even to entertain the thought of doing so. So why do so many people think of freedom in terms of making choices? In some cases because they believe – wrongly – that unless I *choose* to do a certain act, and am able – free – to make the choice not to do it, I cannot be held responsible for my actions. I can be absolved from blame only if I do wrong when I have no choice, as when someone has spiked my drink or given me a drug of which I know nothing and could know nothing until it is too late. Of course, if a more or less virtuous agent finds himself in the (very Augustinian) position of having to choose a course which he knows he will regret, his action is hardly voluntary, though Augustine will, rightly, hold him responsible for it. He will discuss this problem further in the next chapter.

Our Augustine knows of accounts of freedom as choice, but believes that I am less free when I need to *decide* whether this act is right or wrong; more free when I just know that it is right or wrong and act accordingly. He also knows that there are significant implications for the structure, or rather non-structure, of the moral world itself if we accept choice's overriding importance: First, as he will explain, because we ignore the signification of the kind of choices we make, or at least subordinate it to our 'ability' and 'right' to choose. In an extreme case that would imply that it is more important that I have the 'right' – we shall return to Augustine's attitude to rights more generally in Chapter 7 – to kill my child than that I not kill the child. In such a case Augustine also indicates the second and greater oddity about the apotheosis of choice. It implies not only that the mere exercise of my will (ultimately, it would seem, to survive) is what matters, but that we must reject any radical distinction between right and wrong, good and bad – unless we can all *agree* on what is good and bad, better and worse, and choose accordingly. That is not likely to happen.

In the present chapter Augustine will discuss why he has the priorities he has, what are the implications of his position – in the contemporary world he will need to defend this against common opinion – and how it has come about that so many people would assume that he (and many other earlier thinkers) are wrong in the matter.

The difference, of course, is that Augustine's position was established in a theistic universe. In his view, we human beings need God's assistance to perform any good action. Yet he will argue that we do not need to invoke God to show that by our unaided efforts we cannot guarantee that we shall always perform (or want to perform) the right action for the right reasons – nor that we shall necessarily know what the right action would be. Accordingly, he will challenge his opponents with three theses: firstly, that freedom to act – absolute autonomy – will not guarantee right action: rather such 'free' acts just are supposed to *be* right action; secondly, that whatever our desires, we can never be autonomous; thirdly, that to be responsible we do not need to be autonomous: to possess absolute (or perhaps any) freedom of choice. In presenting and defending these three challenges, he will be rejecting some major presuppositions of contemporary Western society.

His first point seems blindingly obvious. Only a fool would insist that any human being would always do the right thing for the right reasons even if he knows what the right thing is. Hence, the reformed fool has to rest his case on a claim that if we sincerely *believe* that we are doing the right thing, we are doing the right thing. Every now and again such ideas re-emerge both among theists and secularists – and when supposedly Christian, as in the writings of the late Joseph Fletcher, they often boil down to a confusion between doing the loving thing and doing what we love to do; truth about what the loving thing is thus becomes irrelevant.

Sincerity-talk need not be Christian, and when it is not, it is usually defended by ideas historically promoted by that second writer of *Confessions* we have already met: Jean-Jacques Rousseau claimed – whether crazily or disingenuously – that he always sincerely tried to do good only to be thwarted by the evil society in which he lived. In the course of history there have been countless examples of even more strikingly malevolent behaviour defended by claims about sincerity. Hitler sincerely believed that all Jews should be killed, but he was not therefore a good man: to be a good Nazi does not unpack as being a good man plus being a Nazi, but rather implies being a bad man *because* one is a good Nazi. To do the right thing it is not enough to hold that one is doing the right thing. Consider the diabolical option: 'Evil, be thou my good.'

Augustine will now move to his second thesis – impugning the claim that we can be autonomous first at a purely secular level, then for good measure adding some religious ballast. He will recognize that he is challenging a philosophical tradition that developed especially in the seventeenth century and reached at least its immediate acme in the writings of Immanuel Kant. But Kant's version of the tradition presents – and needs to present – a peculiar account of what it is to be autonomous. To explain that, our Augustine will have to resort to a little more historical enquiry.

Kant's account of autonomy depends on Descartes's version of the theory that the universe consists of both material and immaterial substance, with our minds being immaterial substances inasmuch as they are capable of reasoning. But since that is all they are capable of, if we are to be identified as our minds, then our actions must be guided by abstract, non-emotional ratiocination about what to do with emotions: our loves and hates, desires and fears. The Aristotelian claim that to be virtuous we must have the right kind of emotions seems here to be implausibly ignored. In the previous chapter we have seen our Augustine indicate some of the difficulties engendered by mind as an inert substance, but as yet he has hardly plumbed the depths of the problem. For Descartes's position requires rejection of the highly plausible claims of Plato and Augustine that when we know the truth (or the truth about anything) we must, without any further *inference*, also love that truth.

Kant neglects this side of human experience; rather, he will not allow it to enter into discussion of morality. What is moral is what our rational mind can prescribe as law for all other minds – or persons – as well as for itself. Kant (and his modern disciples like Rawls) supposes that if we could imagine ourselves living behind some kind of curtain such that all knowledge of our particular circumstances (sex, nationality, religion, physical strength, etc.) is excluded, we would be able to tease out the laws that we should commit ourselves and others to obey. Yet in seeking to put ourselves in that position, we have tried to see ourselves as (or turn ourselves into) an impossible, non-human (because over-individualistic) Cartesian 'ego' or 'self' outside space and time. Augustine has no time for any of that: Kant as a typically reductive metaphysician has omitted every aspect of human nature on which Augustine holds we must reflect historically and biographically. Nor is our mind to be construed on the Cartesian model, so on that score alone (and there are others) the kind of autonomy advocated by Kant is inappropriate for human beings, or in a word inhuman! Kant's account of what we are, being wholly erroneous, cannot be used as a basis for constructing what we are to do. It offers no room for accommodating the loves and hatreds that, our Augustine claims now as then, constitute the groundwork of our moral experience.

Thus, Kant's bizarre account of the mind provides no basis for the construction of moral laws. That, Augustine will point out, at least is now widely recognized, but he will note that Kantian 'constructivists' have not yet surrendered: conceding that we do not need Kant's crazy psychology – they will tell Augustine by way of concession – but maintaining that we are still rational enough to subscribe to such a Kantian rule as, for example, that human beings must always be treated as ends, never merely as means. Augustine is not happy with much of that correction either, at least as presented: firstly, because even if we are all similar *qua* potentially rational beings, that gives us no grounds for according ourselves any value; we could be just as *equally* respected if none of us had any value. The reason Kant was able to come up with his conclusion about the value of persons (whether or not merely rational agents) was not that he successfully argued for it but that he inherited it from his heterodox version of Christianity. In any case, since we cannot envisage humans as purely rational beings (in Kant's sense of 'rational'), we have no reason to be influenced by any such apparently fictional entities.

Even so, Augustine's contemporary neo-Kantian antagonists will still not have given up: they will tell him that even if it is wrong to suppose that we are simply reasoning substances, we are still in a position to formulate and obey the seemingly rational ordinances that we prescribe for others and for ourselves. Our Augustine remains unimpressed, observing that if we look at the whole range of human cultures, that claim can be seen to be false. No society is perfect, nor anywhere near perfect. Even if it manages to improve on its predecessors in very specific ways – as we ourselves claim when we argue that liberal democracy is the best form of government human beings have thus far devised – we know that it is still far from perfect. More generally, Augustine will argue that the solution of serious social problems of the past may entail – frequently does entail – the suppression of other aspects of the best life for man in the present and future.

Thus, a society in which the increase in the GDP is the primary goal will hardly provide the best conditions for encouraging the writing of great poetry, nor any more spiritual reflection. Looking at contemporary Western society, Augustine will admit that in the fifth century he overestimated the changelessness of political systems – being in that a prisoner of his age – adding that our official society and the majority of its 'talking heads' deny or play down vital spiritual goods so far achieved or discovered by mankind, and that, whatever its pretensions, it is a philistine and barbarous society which has forgotten so much known good.

Finally, and with regard to the neo-Kantian claim that we can construct what we think of as a rational moral universe, our Augustine will observe that humanity has always proved unequal to such a task and that what we proclaim as rational ideas are often little more than rationalized accounts of our often irrational and ephemeral desires. Neo-Kantians, he will continue, are de facto choice-theorists in disguise; what they have retained of the Kantian system is its worst part, namely that as autonomous beings we have some sort of capacity – hence right – to adjudge a proceeding rational even when it is not. We defer further comment on 'rights' to Chapter 7, here merely noting another immediate objection to be advanced against both Kant himself and his 'constructivist' successors. Just as humans cannot be reduced to rational agents, so morality cannot be reduced to rationality, not only because humans are *not* just calculating machines (this our Augustine has already explained) but because when an atrocity is committed, as is almost universally agreed, it is not an adequate response to say merely that it is irrational. The Holocaust was certainly irrational, but there was far more wrong with it than that – and that 'far more' is what accounts for our moral revulsion when we hear of it.

Why then, our Augustine will ask, is Kantianism, even in more or less debased forms, still so popular among our élites and their more intellectual pupils? As he will realize, there are many factors involved, but among the more obvious is that it conveys a certain consoling 'transcendence' to 'decent' people in an anti-religious and anti-metaphysical age, giving them a welcome pretext for maintaining concepts of duty, indeed of many of the traditional Christian virtues. Its glaring weakness is that it cannot ground these high-minded ideals in anything more than the inventive mind of a hypothetically rational and autonomous humanity; indeed, it specifically denies any need for a transcendental basis for morality.

In ancient times, Augustine will remember, the Stoics advocated something similarly non-transcendental. They, however, based their theory on an admittedly non-transcendental but at least pantheistically divine being, of whom we human beings are mere fragments. Spinoza was the last Westerner seriously to advocate anything similar. In terms of the materialist view of the natural world now widely accepted, the Stoic version of naturalism can no longer be taken seriously.

All that accepted, yet the most serious problem for Augustine – his third thesis – remains to be settled. If we are not to enjoy a degree of something like Kantian autonomy, how can we be held responsible for what we do? A (postmodern) option might be that the notion of responsibility itself derives from a mere confusion or from a hidden bid for power. Augustine will see no reason why that should be the case, and accordingly will need to proceed step by step in a re-examination of the problem of responsibility. He will know, of course, that medieval thinkers, at least as early as Anselm in the eleventh century, were well aware of the difficulty, though they apparently tried to evade what he himself had said (let alone what he had meant) when (in CG) he claimed that the paradigm case of freedom and responsibility, the revealed fall of the angels, can only be explained by accepting that God gave Satan insufficient grace (12.9).

For Anselm, rightly (see especially *On the Fall of Satan*, 2–4), that desperate solution will not do, seeming to make God (or just bad luck) the prime cause of Satan's (and consequentially Adam's) fall. Augustine needs to explain to us why he advanced such an apparently unsatisfactory explanation in the first place and how he might now prefer to modify it – or leave it aside for another lecture -course and concentrate on the more 'human' problem of whether responsibility will not (even cannot) depend on autonomy, at least as autonomy is normally conceived in the twenty-first century. In passing, he can draw attention again to those radically uncharacteristic acts we all perform which seem to indicate that we are not entirely 'programmed' whether for 'good' or 'evil'.

What worried Augustine when he wrote *The City of God* derived from confusion on two levels: one theological, the other philosophical. The theological difficulty will now pose no problem, since Augustine will accept the developed doctrine of the Church that baptism (though necessary for those who understand its importance) is not always necessary for salvation: God is not limited by the sacraments. The philosophical problem concerns omnipotence, and here Augustine will admit that he was less ill-instructed than confused, as lacking the philosophical resources needed to avoid attributing to God's omnipotence an arbitrary character certainly far from his intent – omnipotence being a concept Christians, *qua* monotheists, had to work out for themselves without any help from 'classical' philosophy.

Our Augustine will acknowledge that his anxiety arose because he assumed that an omnipotent God's will cannot be thwarted. He will now recognize that that premise must be erroneous; God's will is indeed thwarted (as he well knew) every time a sin is committed; that is the price God wills to pay for granting a degree of autonomy to his necessarily dependent human beings. And God can hardly be unaware that in granting such autonomy, he accepts the near-certainty that we shall demand (in Kantian mode) to be fully autonomous, at least morally. And there Augustine will add that not only he but his critics have erred, for if laws are to be morally, as distinct from merely legally, binding, they cannot be established by fallible individuals or groups of individuals, however large. To suppose that they can is to yield to his 'favourite' vice, the pride that tends to make us suppose we can be self-creators.

This is no place to propose further revision of Augustine's strictly theological claims; rather he urges us to return to his analysis of the human condition. For although he is now willing to commit himself to a greater degree of moral autonomy than he envisaged in the past, his basic challenge to Kant and all post-Kantians remains. It is an axiom of contemporary secular philosophy – and a corollary of modern accounts of autonomy – that 'ought' implies 'can'. For a secularizing *theologian* that must imply that we ought to – and so can – become divine. Augustine's original claim, advanced against the Pelagians, was that perfect moral behaviour – indeed even moral adequacy – if not beyond our nostalgic imagination is beyond our unaided capacity. Nonetheless, we are all to be called to account for our failures, if we are to be led (or dragged) to God's heaven.

We have to learn, our Augustine will continue, that we must repudiate that evil inheritance of our nature for which we are all (not personally, but 'in Adam', that is as members of the human race: so *Letter 98* and many other texts) responsible, but which, if honest, we can recognize as simple corollary of our existence. Augustine will remind us that he has always maintained, and still will maintain, that 'ought' must be respected even though we know that we cannot do what we ought to do: that, though regrettable, is a fact. To admit our responsibility for ourselves and for others is no more than to admit dependence: theologically a necessary precondition for sanctification. We are in this respect like children who need 'discipline' (including punishment) to overcome their natural weaknesses.

Augustine's challenge is both at the personal and at the legal level. At the legal level he rejects the obviously false but nowadays widely parroted claim that you cannot legislate morality, as well as the claim that if a law is unenforceable it should be removed from the statute book. (He here follows the principle of the Roman law of his day that law intends not only to maintain order but to indicate what will be the case in a just society.) At the personal level he will insist that we need not only a moral ideal but *recognition,* as of a fact, that we frequently find ourselves unable to obey what we recognize to be moral demands. He might quote Robert Browning's platonizing remark (in *Abt Vogler*), 'Ay, but a man's reach should exceed his grasp / or what's a heaven for?' If what we 'ought' to do were reduced to what we *can* do, we should find ourselves in an all but non-existent 'moral' world.

Kantians and others might urge that if we produce the right society and provide all its members with good medical facilities and a good education, we *shall* be able to do what we ought. Augustine might retort that in practice, that idea leads to a lack of children to educate (perhaps to be addressed by bio-experimentation, whatever its results). But be that as it may, he will reject such ideas about education outright. All attempts at moral self-creation are doomed (and to be condemned as *curiositas*). At this point he will be able to refer us to *The Life-Style of the Catholic Church* (1.21.38) on 'false knowledge', where it is argued that many contemporary claims about education are virtual invocations of superstition or magic.

To this, Augustine will add that his opponents have little idea of what a perfect society could be like; then (again) that there is no evidence that highly educated people are more moral than the educationally less fortunate: indeed, their education may fit them out to be merely better rationalizers than otherwise, humanistic education as currently conceived being more likely to produce sophists than serious thinkers; and the so-called educated often at best half-educated, having learned not least to despise many simple goods.

Reverting to the problem of 'punishment', our Augustine will simply deny that we should never punish people because they are not fully responsible. In the case of children – and morally we are all little more, and often less, than children – we do regularly 'punish' them in order to develop in them those right habits which in an age of greater responsibility they will recognize as desirable. Punishment is just when either intended to improve the 'culprit's' character or to serve as a warning to others.

Many young men (and latterly women), Augustine will remind us, are liable to think (as did he) that their parents are old-fashioned at best, fools at worst. But by the time they face the problems of bringing up their own families – if, that is, they are courageous enough to have families – they recognize that 'My parents often talked a lot of sense'. We all, even saints like Peter and Paul – so, for example, JG, 123.5 – are morally weak – even if some are weaker than others. If we are not held 'responsible' for much at least of what we cannot avoid or resist, we shall never be able to learn. Augustine will manage a wry smile at Oscar Wilde's Lord Darlington (*Lady Windermere's Fan*, Act 1), who can resist everything except temptation!

Augustine is thus unshaken in his belief that we exist in a fallen world, and that our moral choices are taken in 'this darkness of social life' (CG, 19.6). In light of our increased scientific knowledge about the age of the world and the origins of our human species, he will recognize that he must abandon certain significant parts of his earlier 'literal' interpretation of *Genesis*: not its positing the notion of a flawed humanity but of a fall specifically from Paradise. Paradise, he now will tell us, is the natural state of human beings, not yet attained but always – since we have been created in God's image and likeness – buried in our subconscious as an ideal to be longed for. Even in Hippo he had thought of it as part of that 'memory of God' (T [14.12.15]) which we retain within us.

Nor is such a 'natural' ideal the best possible state for us, since merely to correct our flaws is to return us to an 'ideal' condition from which we can still 'fall' again. That fallible condition – this, Augustine will recall, he regularly preached in Hippo – is eventually to be superseded in heaven, where we shall no longer need to choose the good but shall simply and inevitably do it: that is, we shall live 'in peace', incapable of doing wrong as God himself is incapable. Sadly, Augustine will allow, in our secularized world, such belief, being dependent on the virtue of hope, is possible only for theists – or their 'fellow-travellers' – since it rests on the thesis of our adoption (through Christ) as God's children.

Unlike Augustine's old congregation in fifth-century Hippo, we cannot securely 'identify' Adam and Eve, but that need not matter, since all that matters is that we have evolved – somehow – from non-moral beings to beings capable of morality – even over time able to become aware of many moral claims our ancestors could not recognize. Which is not to say that we are better than our fathers and mothers; in some ways we may be worse – even much worse – for if there are now more recognizably moral options, if over time we have come to recognize some hitherto disregarded aspects of our society – such as the subordination of women and the institution of slavery – that brings with it the opportunity to default from these newly recognized moral options.

That granted, all that Augustine will now need to say about the fall is that the *Genesis* story tells us that God acted for good but that there is something radically flawed, a 'surd' factor, in human nature. Perhaps that 'surd' factor needs to exist if we are to recognize what existentially we are; perhaps we are, individually and as members of our species, responsible for that 'genetic' flaw, in Augustine's sense of needing to take responsibility. We thus can learn to be better by recognizing our need to be better. That recognition will be painful and Augustine will still describe it in traditionally Old Testament terms as chastisement, as part of our 'penal condition' (*The Gift of Perseverance* 12.29).

Back in Hippo, our Augustine adhered to the doctrine that this flaw in human nature was handed down to us even as we were conceived in the womb – albeit he lacked a genetic explanation as to how this could have had happened. Nowadays he will say that 'original sin' is to be seen both in our society and in its ill effects on all of us as individuals – as was recognized in a perverse version by Rousseau. He will claim that our genetic make-up, unique to each of us yet similarly flawed, leaves us liable to an ignorance of the good we can never overcome in the present life and an inability wholly to address our attendant weaknesses of character. He has already commented, he will remind us, on his own weakness in the area of sex and Alypius's weakness for bloodshed and tribalized violence.

Although we cannot record exactly how the flaw in our nature came about, we can point to realities that helped set the scene for it. Our Augustine will cite Aristotle's *Politics* – the famous passage (1.1253a14) in which we read that we differ from social insects in that by the related powers of speech and reasoning we can first recognize what is useful and what is not, hence eventually what is good and just and what is not. Originally we had very primitive ideas of what is good for us and how to achieve it; nevertheless, in formulating some notion, however inadequate, of goodness and justice, we achieved the ability to recognize that at least some humans (beginning with our own immediate family) have similar claims to be treated justly, and that there is also the possibility that what is really useful to us will also be what is just.

When we reached that stage, Augustine will continue, we began to experience the clash between our own short-term interests and what is both better for ourselves in the long run and also tied in to our developing more 'civilized' relations with others: first with those nearest to us, eventually more widely. Now, however, Augustine will warn us that as we expand our horizon, recognizing the clan, then the nation as fit subjects for just treatment, we should not forget that justice must still pertain to the family; the last thing we should become is 'lovers of mankind' who treat actual humans badly and are even willing to sacrifice them on behalf of an abstract Humanity. If we do that, he concludes, we shall have forgotten the importance to be attributed to our personal relationships and to those of others.

In developing such a realistic approach to our expanding sense of what is implicit in our being moral, our Augustine can recall, with satisfaction, that he has rid himself of a theological incubus that bore hard on his earlier self and on great number of his Christian successors, namely that he no longer has to bear the burden of explaining violent acts as planned and upheld by the God of the Old Testament. With modern philology at his disposal, he recognizes that the Old Testament – unlike in this the Qur'an – is not to be held in a literal sense to be the word of God, rather what earlier generations of Hebrews *thought* of as God's literal words and commands. He can confirm this interpretation by noting how in the later parts of the Old Testament, perhaps most typically in Isaiah, God's 'prophets' – those who speak for him – have learned to prefer the sacrifice of a pure heart not only to such human sacrifice as Abraham had supposed himself commanded to enact, but to any blood- sacrifice.

So now Augustine can remind the 'autonomists' of Adam and Eve, arguing that when our race began to be human, we entered upon a history of mental activity that could, and did, lead to our present moral condition and can lead us beyond it. Most of us now, he will continue, believe that even though we flounder hopelessly trying to explain it, we live in what has been dubbed 'moral space' – even though we differ wildly when asked as to that space's contents. Nevertheless, by the mere fact of such a belief, we show that we are not unaware of the importance of what we 'ought' to do, as of our inability to live up to what in our better moments we recognize as principles of a good life. We are radically divided, and when divided, we often choose the wrong, even the irrational, course, thus making our minds, as Augustine will wryly observe, the Humean slaves of our passions. Even so, when we do that, we may *feel* that we are doing wrong – and Augustine will note once more that Aristotle spent much time, in book seven of his *Nicomachean Ethics*, examining such feelings in the context of what he calls *acrasia* – weakness of will. ('I really should not be doing this', the man said, as he drained the bottle of vodka.)

Thus, our Augustine will tell us that he has broadened the scope of Aristotle's analysis; we are all, all too often, even though not all to the same degree, subject to massive weakness of will, and when we realize that this really is *weakness*, we may try to pretend that the wrong we have done against our will is someone else's fault. Adam put the blame on Eve, Eve on the serpent. We rationalize (like Rousseau), and mutter, as Adam to God, 'Not me Gov.'. For in this life, as Augustine has already noticed, so soon as we begin to reason we also begin to rationalize – and the better educated we are, the more sophisticated the rationalizings we can develop. Yet many intelligent 'lay' people can recognize the transparency of this rationalizing: what many professors claim to believe may seem to them so contrary to common sense that – professors or public intellectuals apart – only an immature seventeen-year-old would attempt to defend anything so obviously inane!

Our Augustine thus reiterates that much crazy philosophical speculation derives from the arrogant desire to rationalize away our faults (including our intellectual faults), our moral weaknesses, even our ignorance: that, as he pointed out in *The City of God* (first at 7.25), even those philosophers (like Porphyry) who are most successful as metaphysicians refuse to admit that they have reached the limits of their understanding and then – to evade recognizing and accepting their own ignorance – fall back on superstition: as in our modern world, it may be, on the superstition of scientism. And Augustine will not be surprised that the more autonomous we try to be, the more we fall into error of that kind.

4

The State: Persecution, War, Justice – and Regret

Augustine's readers have often complained that he says little about practical politics and political thought, concentrating instead on delineating the Christian who may – perhaps regrettably – be drawn into politics. There is justification for that complaint, for Augustine himself says that without justice kingdoms are merely higher brigandages (CG, 4.4): in this committing himself to having ideas about forms of political governance. Restored for the twenty-first century, he will have to pay more attention to political theories and discussion of the merits of different sorts of régimes, not least because he will understand that political writers, especially Machiavelli and Hobbes, are among the Founding Fathers of a modernity of which, as we have already seen, he will be radically critical.

As is true of all social and political thinkers, Augustine's ideas about government and the law were developed against the background of the political and social world in which he lived. By the time he died, the Roman Peace that formed that background was coming to an end, though its spirit, often in an idealized version, was to live on for centuries. It was a harsh but comparatively predictable world; 'discipline' is one of Augustine's favourite themes, whether in the family or in the State. It implies that order, whether familial or public, must in the last resort be maintained by force, even though that might seem to contradict a Christian ideal of society.

Indeed, that ideal is necessarily unattainable after the fall; we now live in a brutal world where the 'lust to dominate' is everywhere visible – in relations between the sexes, between fathers and sons, between rulers and subjects – and power is liable to be abused;

yet we cannot dispense with it (CG, 15.7.1). Therefore, in the family the father's role is to maintain 'domestic peace' (CG, 19.16). Obedience, whether to secular or ecclesiastical authorities, must be upheld, since without it, society is reduced to unmitigated savagery. In the fifth century that necessary reliance on force had already led Augustine into difficulties, not least about the persecution of heretics. Even so, he never urged that pagans be subject to forced baptism nor Jews pressured to convert; indeed, Jews should be allowed to practise their religion in peace; they will be converted in the Last Times. Meanwhile, they serve both as reminder of the continuing importance of God's word in the Old Testament and as warning to those who deny the divinity of Christ.

And despite briefly succumbing to triumphalism, Augustine never urged the sacralization of the State, and would be appalled by our contemporary totalitarian projects, including those in liberal guise. He believes that politics, a merely human activity, would have been unnecessary had it not been for the fall; at best, it can only secure the most 'peaceful' society possible in humanity's fallen condition and functions as a rough-and-ready protection against vice rather than a promoter of virtue (as the Greek philosophers had preferred to see it). The State bears no comparison with the 'City' of God and, unlike individuals and families, has no part in salvation.

When our twenty-first-century Augustine looks back on his support for the persecution of heretics – that particularly sad group who have been offered the Truth but perverted it – he will ponder the matter from a standpoint both psychological and historical, which will enable him to recognize how his earlier attitude, though not entirely indefensible, is philosophically and theologically incoherent. Nevertheless, he will continue to insist, against modern appeasers of evil and naive idealists, that in thinking about the good of society, the first essential is to acknowledge the *weakness* of human nature and how that can be mitigated: often and always regrettably only by force.

Such reflection in its turn will enable him to assert the continuing relevance of many of his more negative views of public life – not least of military life – as also to comment on the modern claim that the least worst form of government is some version of our contemporary liberal democracies. He will have to put more emphasis on the obvious fact that some rulers – and by extension some régimes – are very much better than others; that some may even represent a genuine human achievement, as do works of art and all those strictly 'human' accomplishments he praised at the end of the *City of God* (22.24).

It is informative, however, to start with religious persecution, if we are to give Augustine the chance to explain how his earlier views can be corrected on his own principles. For this course will simultaneously reveal how his corrected as well as many of his original ideas can have much to teach us. For although Augustine was confused about persecution, his reasons for being so were far from trivial. Hence, as so often, the first step in our enquiry must be historical; offering brief comment on why attitudes towards persecution have changed since the fifth century. That will again point us towards the problems about rights that will require more detailed attention in a later chapter.

With Constantine's division of the Roman Empire into (broadly) Latin-speaking and Greek-speaking regions, Christendom became divided, with Augustine being, as we have seen, both for better and for worse, on the Latin side of this divide. With the Reformation, Western Christendom would be further fragmented, and the fragmentation is ever increasing. For the first century or so after the Reformation, many members of the larger competing groups came increasingly, if naively, to believe that their respective orthodoxies could be promoted and enforced only with the help of the State. They looked for the support of princes whose motives for backing one party rather than another varied from more genuine religious conviction to a dominant urge to subordinate all religion – not merely ritual and liturgy but also doctrine – to themselves.

Those who thought of themselves as statesmen increasingly wished the State to be autonomous. At the same time, many of those who, reasonably or not, had felt oppressed in the past world came to think of submission to one only of the two medieval 'swords' – to the State and not also to a dominant Church – as the better option, perhaps pointing to a greater autonomy not just for the State but for themselves. Perhaps some form of decreasingly Christian – even non-theistic – State might prove the only protection against persecution by one or other of the religious factions of the day – or allow 'right-thinkers' more effectively to persecute those seen as more diabolically inspired.

Thus power, of the State and of its members, triumphed over dogmatic certainties, and new theories of subjective rights expanded rapidly. Such theories might have been developed from accounts of

man in the image of God centuries earlier, even, as we shall see, in
Augustine himself, but hardly were, rights being in medieval times
viewed as the rights of powers such as kings, bishops, lords, guilds
against one another. Subjective individual rights only emerged at a
late stage – and hesitantly, as with Las Casas in Mexico – as heralded
and progressive forerunners of the increasing dechristianizing
of Europe in the eighteenth century. Yet although at the political
level Christianity was by then on the defensive, mere power is no
index to truth or right; nor should we forget that those who first
challenged the old certainties about persecuting 'heretics' (however
defined) were Christians themselves, and that they drew strength
from their Christianity.

Nevertheless, the metaphysical weaknesses of many varieties
of post-Reformation Christianity led to the originally Christian
humanitarian impulses of the seventeenth and eighteenth centuries
transforming themselves into purely 'secular' conclusions about
subjective rights. These, falsely taken to be self-evidently factual,
reveal themselves as in many ways the intellectually disreputable
bastards of Christian ancestors. Thus when our Augustine shall
visit New England, he will observe how Congregationalist
churches have become Unitarian, with their headquarters in
Boston, then – logically if, as Russell observed, Unitarians believe
'in one God at most' – have morphed into the now-fashionable
anti-Church stances of intellectuals in that part of the world. In
more British lands, Augustine will notice how in the nineteenth
and twentieth centuries the sons of Methodist circuit preachers or
of the Manse became lay apostles of what he will denounce as an
illusory and metaphysically indefensible secular, often 'socialist',
utopian dream.

Looking up all this, our Augustine may well ponder as to where
he ran into intellectual trouble, notably about persecution, and how
he now can escape from it. He will soon realize that he should
have attended more closely to the dignity of the human person: a
concept in many ways alien to the spirit of the late Roman Empire.
Yet even then he had a certain awareness of it and knew that it can
only depend on the doctrine that we are created in the image of
God; that is – as after a little hesitation he expressed it – as images
of the Trinity. But in what does this dignity consist, and how does
it relate to that account of freedom as the capacity only to seek the
good which, as we have seen, he needs only minimally to revise in

a more 'libertarian' direction – if only to allow that one man, even one pagan, really is morally better than another?

Yet even in accepting that more libertarian account, Augustine will still refuse to abandon the idea of man's weakness and need to rely on help from God – and more immediately from God's representatives, the Catholic bishops, provided they behave as real bishops and are able to play the role for which they are intended. The question arises: What kind of properly Christian help can bishops (and others) give sinners so that they may more readily reach their spiritual goal? Are *any* means allowable, provided they are feasible? If so, then religious persecution, especially of heretics, is sometimes justified; if not, there will be good reason to reject all violent means of bringing the sheep back to the fold.

Augustine will be obliged to admit that the primary reason for ruling out all religious persecution is that it contradicts the image of God in the individual whose essence *qua* image is bound up with the awesome capacity to be at least minimally able to *choose* for himself. Before accepting that, Augustine will not unreasonably ask himself whether in rejecting the use of force on heretics, we shall lose sight of the dreadful significance of right and wrong choices, of being numbered among the sheep or among the goats. Yet he will remember that when discussing pre-fallen Satan and Adam, his approach was more optimistic (CG, 22.1):

> God bestowed on those intellectual natures [the angels] a power of free choice such that they might forsake God if they wished to do so: might, that is, relinquish their blessedness and receive misery as the immediate consequence. And he foreknew that, in their pride, some of the angels would indeed wish to be self-sufficient for their own blessedness, and hence would forsake their true Good. Yet He did not deprive them of the power to do this; for he judged it an act of greater power and goodness to bring good even out of evil than to exclude the existence of evil...... and God also made man righteous, with the same freedom of will..... God foreknew that man would sin...yet he did not deprive man of his freedom of will.... (Dyson's translation slightly adapted)

Even if Augustine thinks that man's dignity as an image of God requires us to learn the eschatological facts of life – and thus secure our ultimate perfection – the hard way, he must now allow not only that human dignity requires a rather more libertarian 'will', but also that it is within God's power to restore such a 'will' in our present life. Only if he is unwilling to accept such an estimate of what is required to ensure that the integrity of the image of God is protected, despite the sin of Adam, will Augustine be right to advocate physical or psychological violence to secure religious orthodoxy. And if he does accept it, he will recognize that his own account of what human dignity demands must apply in our fallen state as it did for unfallen Adam and Eve.

Thus religious freedom is essential unless God's fashioning of man's original dignity was in error – which Augustine cannot and so will not maintain. That accepted, and man being in a better condition if as yet he has a certain option of choosing the bad, what remains to be determined is what pressure to conform can appropriately be put on heretics or others and what not. Augustine might review consequentialist arguments – in a later chapter we shall return to what he must regret as his limited consequentialism – about the possible benefit to the children of those persecuted into orthodoxy. Nevertheless, he will be unable to evade what he had always recognized: that we cannot be *compelled into love* of the good, only into an enforced and inhuman submission seemingly unworthy of our divinely proposed destiny. When we love aright, our 'wills' are prepared by God (*Proverbs* 8.35); they are not forced.

In the twenty-first century many would try to resolve Augustine's problem about persecution by appealing to human rights. Christians, but not non-believers, can follow Locke in developing the doctrine of humans being in the image of God to assert that we are possessors of rights given by God, indeed that their possession is an essential feature of our being created, each of us individually, in the divine image. But although much modern rights-talk will fail to impress an Augustine well aware of the difficulties it entails, he will find an indirect approach more difficult to discount.

That approach depends on the philosophically more plausible notion that rights-claims, even if theologically based, are intelligible only in terms of the older position that our duty – after loving God above all things – is secondarily to attend to our *own* virtue; that is, to love ourselves in the proper sense, and to have that respect for ourselves as formed in the image of God which is the only basis on which love of others can be built (T, 14.14.18). Only when concerned with such a properly ordered self-love can we love our neighbour – also, of course, in God – *as ourselves*, thus recognizing *his* or *her* 'rights'. However, Augustine will defer a more detailed account of rights to a later chapter.

Thus, New Augustine will challenge Old Augustine precisely where he underestimated what is required to maintain and promote our own and therefore others' moral well-being. In that it will not only be Old Augustine who is challenged, for the standard assumption in antiquity and in many succeeding centuries among both Christians and pagans was that brutal treatment can be imposed on the wicked without causing moral harm to the punishing agent. Our Augustine will no longer allow that assumption to go unchallenged, once it is seen to be an empirical mistake. No one is more convinced than Augustine that his tragically bleak account of the human condition is empirically based.

When Augustine allowed both that we need executioners and that such people are the scum of the earth (*On Order* 2.4.12), he should have recognized that even such scum cannot be employed merely as functionaries to their own detriment – which is further to the detriment of those who employ them. In their case too, human dignity should be respected. Now he must also recognize precisely *qua* bishop that he should not persecute: less perhaps in the first instance because he might infringe on someone's rights (though we can certainly argue that he would) than because, by persecuting, he not only tries to enforce love but by brutalizing himself diminishes his own hope of attaining the moral excellence and happiness which, with God's aid and in accordance with God's original intentions, he is in obedience *and* love bound to pursue and promote.

Problems like that posed by the need for executioners bring us to wider aspects of Augustine's account of justice, and its application in both civil and military life. For his ideas about the enforcement of order were excessively top-down, the most striking example being that subordinates are simply to obey orders: thus the executioner (in civil society) and the rank-and-file soldier are licensed to carry out any commands, however brutal (and they would regularly include torture) without being held responsible. Perhaps, he will admit, he should have looked more carefully at the different degrees of responsibility to be assigned to the different levels of organized structures of command.

Although in characteristically ancient style the fifth-century Augustine largely ignored systemic injustices – what Catholics now call 'structures of sin' – like slavery which he thought inevitable in our fallen world, about those senior or middle-rank officials who issue savage commands, he was and will remain fearfully unambiguous. We recall the famous passage from the *City of God* (19.6) in which he has described the situation of a judge compelled in the course of his legal duties to torture people who may in fact be innocent. (In antiquity slaves were routinely subject to judicial torture; in Roman times this might be inflicted on the orders of a bishop acting as magistrate.)

So was the plea 'I was just obeying orders' acceptable in the ancient Augustine's public world? Sometimes, certainly, as we have seen, yet perhaps not always. In *On Human Responsibility* (1.5.11) he opines that unjust laws are not laws and hence should not be obeyed. The problem with that is how to determine, without bias, whether a supposed law is unjust. As far as we know, Augustine (and other Christians of his day) was clear about this only in the case of pagan laws which prevented or inhibited Christian practice and proselytizing – and it is perhaps only to such laws that Augustine refers in *On Human Responsibility*.

If that is the case, Augustine will now need to modify his stance, based as it was on only very limited reflection on forms of government. The ancient Christian position on obedience to the State was developed largely because the pre-Constantinian Empire (the basic structures of which continued in the Christian era) was hostile to Christianity: 'unjust' laws were therefore those that the State proposed specifically as anti-Christian. Yet even if Augustine would not actively encourage Count von Stauffenberg to develop and activate his plan to blow up Hitler, he would hardly have been complacent about accepting (for example) Nazi laws aimed at persecuting and eliminating Jews (these, as we have seen, he specifically urged should be protected) or other unwelcome groups.

If that is right, Augustine will have to review the concept of an 'order' that underpins his view of the acceptability of 'just obeying orders'. That will point not only to a different account of proper obedience but more widely to where he declined to go in the fifth century. Now he will consider forms of government which allow for minority rights, reject the use of torture against 'heretics' (political or ecclesial) and do not degenerate into a dictatorship of the rulers, whether or not they happen to be the majority – the 'people' – as they claimed to be in ancient Athens or Revolutionary France. But he will defer that further discussion in favour of returning to the situation of those civil and military officials – including bishops – who *are* to be held responsible, at least by God, for their actions and commands.

Augustine's world is parlous for office holders, though less widely so than our own news-sodden and apparently democratic society where every citizen, indeed every resident, is to be held to some degree responsible for violent and unjust acts in the public sphere, even those in faraway lands calling for his (even irresponsible) compassion. Nevertheless, in Augustine's world, whether then or now, officials, military and civil live in the characteristic conditions of a fallen society, being often obliged to perform actions they would not wish to perform: to choose, that is, when they would prefer not to choose (and where not-to-choose is regarded as dishonourable). They will have to have dirty hands, lest worse befall. For Augustine will now recognize more clearly than he once did – albeit he was far from *unaware* of it – that all of us from time to time find ourselves in circumstances where we would wish not to be where in fact we find ourselves, for reasons whether public or private – but there is no reasonable way out.

That entails that feelings of deep regret, even shame, must be the mark of the man who takes Augustine's account seriously in his daily life, whether public or private. Thus modern Americans, if conscientious, can hardly avoid regretting that in an election they have had to choose between 'Miss Abortion USA' and a man who wanted to make torture official government policy. If Augustine is right about the kind of situation in which we too often find ourselves, we have to recognize, he still concludes, that this is one of the most obvious marks of our penal condition: an effect, that is, of the 'fall'. From such situations we cannot escape, and our sense of regret can only profitably take the form of praying for God's forgiveness (he gives one example from many at E, 21.78). Regret is to be transformed into repentance, even for crimes for which (in accordance with the theory of original sin) we are not 'personally' responsible. None of us will be able to avoid such dilemmas in our present life, and whether or not we regard Augustine as right about what we should do when we find ourselves so confronted, he is certainly right to identify the ubiquitous nature of a dilemma that presents itself in myriad forms. Military activity provides the most informative, but far from the only, examples. To cause collateral damage in warfare is a case of dirty hands, but abandoning a just cause or losing a more or less just war may often be the only alternative.

The case of the executioner has introduced us to the fact that State service, and not only in the profession of arms, can involve the shedding of blood. Nevertheless, we should not be surprised when Augustine continues to maintain that he was right – when approached by a General Boniface, grown weary of killing, mutilating and inflicting pain in the course of his daily duties and wondering about becoming a monk – to reply: 'No. We need loyal and competent generals' (L, 189, 220). The word 'need' is a key to much of Augustine's political thought, not only about individual military behaviour but also about the morality of warfare, indeed of the whole of public life.

There is no just war *theory* in Augustine (though this was attributed to him in later centuries); indeed, he does not say very much about warfare and what he does say is primarily in the context of defending the God of the Old Testament (as we have seen) against allegations of barbarism and savagery. Augustine's view of warfare more generally is characterized by this defensive stance. He seems to have concluded – cautiously enough – that the only just wars are either those directly ordered by God (as with the apparently genocidal wars of Moses and Joshua) – for God could not give unjust commands – or those rare others which the godly ruler (such as the emperor Theodosius) wages for God's obvious purposes rather than his own glory.

Yet in the modern world, as we have seen, Augustine should not need to defend the justice of the Old Testament God in the case of his 'commands' or supposed commands to Moses and Joshua. Thus, his thinking can develop along less exegetical and more pastoral – indeed more philosophical – lines. In traditional just war theory a distinction is made between reasons for going to war – this should be to use proportionate force in self-defence or to rectify obvious injustices – and the behaviour of soldiers in any war, however justly declared. Augustine could see that even in the most justified warfare evil acts are liable to be committed even by the 'just' party – and evil motives such as the desire for revenge are liable frequently to prevail. The just party's troops may be so enraged at their opponents' atrocities that they react unjustly themselves, as when during the Second World War captured members of the Waffen-SS were shot out of hand. Such situations demonstrate that the purity of motive Augustine demands if a war (or any other action) is to be deemed 'just' is regularly and inevitably lacking.

That none of this makes Augustine a pacifist is hardly surprising. Even before the Christianization of the empire there were Christian 'accommodationists' willing to perform both civil and military service for the State. But the conversion of Constantine compelled Christian thinkers to take the problem of 'dirty hands' much more seriously: some of them (like Lactantius, the one-time chronicler of the foul deaths of persecuting emperors) changed their thinking completely under the new régime. Without the fall there would have been no warfare: as we are, some wars, even though they cannot be waged according to principles of strict justice, are nevertheless necessary. Some, that is, are *less unjust* – perhaps very much less unjust – than others. Only God is just (and the rare-as-a-phoenix ultra-godly), and only such can conduct a 'just' war justly.

Augustine's stance here is again Platonic (and perhaps to a degree Stoic). All virtuous action falls short of the virtue (in this case Justice) itself – and Plato's Form of Justice has become a 'transcendental' (to use an anachronistic terminology); that is a divine attribute. Augustine has in effect distinguished between reasons for going to war and wrongful actions committed during the war itself. Virtually no one can declare war for entirely just and good reasons (even where the war is necessary), and no one can expect that either he or his soldiers will behave justly (whether in act or in motive) during the hostilities. That again is part of our 'penal' condition, or at least (for secularists) of the condition of our evolved nature.

The Stoic aspect of all this, though less clear, is visible. The Stoics divide all behaviour into two classes: virtuous acts from perfect motives, which are almost never achieved (indeed the good man is as rare as the phoenix), and vicious acts (these include everything strictly non-virtuous). Within the vicious class, however, there are behaviours that point us either towards virtue or towards vice. 'Better' (technically 'preferred') actions are 'according to nature' and would include doing what is necessary to defend oneself; 'just' warfare would fall under this head. Augustine knew this theory and might have had it in mind as an anthropological supplement to the more metaphysical Platonic account of justice: that is, as often elsewhere in Augustine's philosophical world, the Platonists help us understand the metaphysical structure of the universe and its maker; the Stoics help us understand many aspects of human action and motivation.

All the topics our Augustine has so far treated in this chapter are in some sense political, but he has said little as yet about the best form of constitution, a topic which most of his ancient predecessors and many of his more recent successors have treated at length. Indeed, the absence of this theme in the original writings of Augustine led his medieval successors to construct a more developed political theory for him, nowadays dubbed 'political Augustinianism', though its claim to be genuinely Augustinian can be readily challenged.

We may wonder once more why – assumptions about 'eternal Rome' apart – Augustine had so little to say about possible constitutions. Apparently he thought the question unimportant since the best principles would produce the result that all political communities in a fallen world will be in many ways corrupt, if not a culturally bound assertion that the autocratic government of the sort the Roman Empire provided – whether in its pagan or its Christianized forms – would be the only practical option for future generations. (Indeed, were he looking at our contemporary Middle East, he might well want to argue that some sort of hopefully benevolent dictatorship – more like the Roman Empire at its best – would be the best constitution on offer at least for those parts.)

Our Augustine will realize that on constitutions he was too simplistic now that the plurality of political societies debated by the great Greek political thinkers – notably Plato and Aristotle – has returned in very different guise. In our Western world one of them – a liberal form of democracy based on a controlled capitalism – is widely held to be anything between virtually perfect and the least worst option. The latter evaluation is certainly nearer to what Augustine will now believe to be the case. So our final question must be how, in the light of his basic outlook on politics, he will view our contemporary liberal democracy. As a full-scale reply to such a request would extend over many pages, he will prefer only to critique some fundamental assumptions about our society, leaving more general questions about the importance of rights for separate treatment.

Four themes he will consider are: equality for all under the law, both male and female citizens being treated equally; tolerance, which he has already discussed in connection with persecution; the *de jure* or *de facto* separation of Church and State; the underlying apotheosis of choice and its consequent possible implications for totalitarianism, nihilism or a mindless conventionalism. Treating of the liberal State, he will, of course, begin by reminding us that those who run it are not immune to original sin, and that this is revealed in the marked tendency of liberal States to develop and retain totalitarian features. There is truth in the old saying that all history is the history of élites, and liberal States are run by élites of liberal stamp.

Not being a fool, our Augustine will admit that we understand more than he did about some of the differences between the sexes, though he will add that we do not know as much as we think and moreover have forgotten some important realities of which our ancestors, including his parishioners in Hippo, were often aware. But, as we have already observed, a dominant, though erroneous, idea in antiquity was that if two individuals in a living species are different, then one is superior to the other. Hence men and women being different, men must in some general way be superior to women, even if in some respects women are superior. Augustine thinks that women's capacity for love is greater (hence Mary Magdalene was the first witness to the Resurrection: S, 229.1), not least because, as Origen in particular had emphasized, in respect of its relation to God every soul is 'female' and receptive. He was nonetheless inclined to fall back on the more conventional view that male superiorities will trump any female superiorities, and that would have governed his attitude to women in public life.

The axiom about superiority and inferiority is ill founded, being another exemplar of comparing apples with oranges. Rather it seems to be the case that most men are superior to most women in some respects, while most women are superior to most men in other equally or more important respects. Augustine will recognize that, since love is the basic virtue, and inseparable from any possible knowledge of God. Even in antiquity some held that men and women are equally 'human' and therefore potentially of equal value, albeit with different capacities. A third thesis (probably envisaged by Plato as well as others including some Christians) is that sexual differences are bodily only; women are 'male in mind'. That view our Augustine will rule out, since the differing hormonal systems of men and women affect the mind, bearing out Aristotle's conviction that where there are bodily differences there will be psychological differences: but, he will now recognize, differences are not (as Aristotle at *Politics* (1.1260a13)) necessarily superiorities and inferiorities.

Like many other Catholics, our Augustine will now propose a theory of complementarity – thus involving himself in the difficulties that arise in cashing that notion out and which it is not our concern to explore here. Yet even if we grant him complementarity, he will now have to accept the capacity (not of course the necessity) of women to be effective in all forms of public life and service, recognizing what has become axiomatic – at least since the French Revolution: the abandonment of the old distinction placing women in the private, men in the public sphere.

Yet though the liberal-democratic State assumes the equality of the sexes, it tends towards assuming their *identity*: that is, that the differences between them are matters primarily of 'gender': that is of societal expectations with no significant basis in nature. Since our political society is democratic, 'equality' will tend to reduce itself to the pursuit (even to impossible lengths) of identity, which in effect means homogenization (to this Augustine will turn in a later chapter). Needless to say he will be opposed to this tendency, urging that democratic would-be 'transhumanists', *qua* self-creators, are (yet again) self-deceivers who even if they do not admit that they are created by God, should certainly allow that they did not and could not create themselves. It is one thing to deny the existence of God; quite another to arrogate God's power to oneself.

The liberal-democratic State is expected not only to be tolerant of such a mindless attitude but even to promote it, on the grounds that people are to be encouraged to be what they choose to be! So our Augustine must turn to principles not only about limits of toleration but also about the clash of rights. He will continue to maintain the right of the unborn to be born, now in the face of those who say that the mother has the right – even the absolute and unlimited right – to kill it, and to allow others, 'Planned Parenthood', to butcher it for its parts. He will point out that this clash cannot be dismissed as a mere illusion of anti-abortionists, for it can (and does) arise equally for new-born and even older children. He will consider – and rebut – the doctor who says that if only we could get over our hang-ups about infanticide we should have no problem with abortion, pointing out that such cases will normally resolve themselves when challenged into questions less of ideology – let alone of rational argument – than of that 'lust for power' which is merely concealed by the fig- leaf of liberal values such as toleration and diversity. If our liberal élites can determine the right to kill, that is because, in political terms, they have assumed the power to silence those who oppose such killing, or to put them out of business.

For the liberal-democratic State is tolerant only up to a point, and intolerant not only of those who want to destroy it by violence (a stance which is clearly defensible), but also of those who wish to uphold their consciences against the politically correct fads of the moment, even when lethal. Augustine will observe this in attempts to compel doctors and midwives to assist in medical practices they regard as grossly immoral: not only claiming to eliminate from their position those impelled in conscience to resist such options, but even to ensure that such are not allowed into the medical profession at all. He will argue that he would have opposed such aberrations in the past and finds them no less morally offensive for being perpetrated with the blessing of a perverted liberal-democratic theory. In this he will simply be denying the ideological axiom that man is (should be, or could be) the measure of all things.

Would Augustine then suppose that the Church should control the State as in the Middle Ages when theocracy was still an option? Though he might recall such a possibility nostalgically, he will recognize it as unacceptable not only de facto but on his own principles, lest those who would be the theocrats be themselves infected by the 'lust to dominate'. Even in the fifth century, Augustine had no confidence that theocracy could or would work. Church and State must be substantially distinct, with neither the State running the Church nor the Church the State, but he will add that this does not entail that the Church should not be free to criticize the State, to condemn its behaviour when it judges that to be necessary and to resist all liberal attempts to annul its obligation to criticize.

As Socrates was executed by the Athenians because he criticized their laws and mentality, so Augustine will expect the Church in contemporary liberal-democratic society to come under sustained attempts to undermine and destroy it. Totalitarian behaviour is even more hateful in a world view in which God exists than if he did not: the totalitarian ruler is in effect claiming to be god, and the liberal will tend to the totalitarian. Moreover, Augustine will expect to be persecuted and silenced from telling the inconvenient truth in such matters: such criticism undermines the power of the rulers and of the 'intellectual' culture that sustains them.

Criticizing secular abuse of that principle of the separation of Church and State which he will now feel obliged to accept, our

Augustine will defy not only the liberal establishment insofar as it tends to deny freedom of conscience but also democracy itself insofar as in exalting politicians, totalitarian or other, it worships idols only less implausible than its celebrities. From Scripture (*Matthew* 12.44) he will remind us that, the conscience allayed, seven devils will enter in.

Our Augustine can challenge us further, asking whether, given that our present society is, *yes*, liberal, it is also authentically democratic. Yes, democratic structures are in place; he asks whether they allow for genuine choices of policies honestly laid out, or rather the gulling of the voting public. Answering his own question he will reply that there is a certain level of democracy in place – much as came about in ancient Athens – but the realities of re-election and the politicians' lust to dominate – they pervert the word 'ambition' into something acceptable – largely prevent them from speaking truthfully to the public, the more so since the public may often not like to hear the truth.

Nor will he find it difficult to come up with examples. In Great Britain he may instance the inability of any politician – and the reasons for that inability – to solve what is known as 'the crisis in the National Health Service' – or even to admit their own responsibility for it. More widely he will ask about claims that Islam is a religion of 'peace', when peace for Islam is the peace imposed on the subjugated, just as Mohammed himself, as the Qur'an and the Muslim 'traditions' depict him, was a violent subjugator. Augustine, thumbing through the pages of Tacitus – a pagan historian whom previously he seems not to have read – will find comparable abuse of the rather similar 'peace' as enforced by the Roman emperors who make a desert and call it peace (*Agricola* 30).

His criticism of the political classes is the more serious, Augustine will insist, in that he identifies Truth with Christ and regards lying, as also that version of it known as 'spinning' – and especially in matters of religion – as damnably pernicious since blasphemous of the God who is Truth. And he will detect lying, or at the least wilful deceiving built into our society far beyond the self-seeking speeches of the politicians. Having acknowledged that all history (that is, political history) is the history of élites, he knows that frequently in a democratic society politicians are called on to act instantly on very complex problems which will seriously affect the whole society they purport to represent. In so doing, however, they rely necessarily on small groups of highly intelligent – and highly paid – men and women, who have earned or bought their ear, and may have their own often far from honest or democratic agendas. And that, Augustine will affirm, is only the beginning of the problem; for the politicians will fear being misrepresented – or even represented truthfully – by the media. Fear, he will conclude, except fear of the Lord, is a bad counsellor.

Having outlined such criticisms, our Augustine will ask how far a public may be self- deluding about their elected government. True democracy, he will point out, is not only about the establishing of democratic processes (such as elections); as important for it must be the pursuit of democratic ends. If an end is held democratically acceptable merely insofar as it is willed by an ignorant and misguided public, democracy reduces itself to a contriving authoritarianism, pandering to agreed injustices or to ever-changing fads with no basis but the nihilism of absolute choice.

5

Against Political Panaceas

As we saw in the previous chapter, the historical Augustine made no attempt to delineate an ideal constitution, making it clear that he had no enthusiasm for any particular form of political society, albeit he supposed nominally Christian structures would have certain advantages. For him what matters most in public life is the maintenance of law and order: that is, of whatever even tolerably peaceful life a given society can manage. But not only did would-be theocrats of the Middle Ages try to develop his moral ideas into some kind of Christian polity, but even a number of ex-Christians and post-Christians have tried to achieve what he thought impossible: the formulation and, hopefully, the construction of some 'best' society on earth. Some of the first to do this in the early modern period – prominent among them both Machiavelli and Hobbes – based their projects on what looks to be a rather Augustinian account of a potentially vicious humanity, most clearly visible in those possessing political power. Thomas More too – as I shall contend a man with little sympathy for political utopias – began his reflections on possibly ideal constructions by accepting a patently Augustinian account of human nature.

Augustine thinks that the very supposition of there being a political panacea is profoundly unchristian, since it assumes man's power for good – his capacity, that is, to reason and to love – to be greater than it is, while the search for panaceas too often leads to the divinization and self-divinization of rulers. Looking back on the twentieth century, he will observe how Fascist and Communist ideologues have attempted to produce what they believed to be perfect societies populated by 'New Men'. What they have actually engineered was the horrifying degradation of those compelled to live under their dictatorships, obey their brutal orders and believe their propaganda – almost as great as that of the apparatchiks who have sought to enforce their commands.

Nor, as we have seen, would Augustine spare liberal democracies run by rulers who pander – or claim to pander – to populist whims. Of course, he recognized that even in pagan times some rulers were better than others: Trajan was a better emperor than Nero. But what does 'better' imply in such a context? Certainly that improvements in society cannot be implemented by revolutionary violence – which may destroy the bad, normally only to replace it by the worse – but only gradually and hesitantly. That is why he will like More's approach to politics, recognizing both the constant need for realism and the inevitable dangers of a course which involves working with very nasty people and tolerating some of their less noxious, even if still undesirable, characteristics. In Roman times he would think of Seneca, the Stoic minister of Nero, and we recall that he told General Boniface that as well as monks we need generals. The ambiguous relationships required of public figures are a recurrent phenomenon; I once heard a diplomat say he always felt strange shaking hands with mass- murderers.

Our Augustine would want to argue that Thomas More, already lecturing on *The City of God* as a young man, got much of the story right about politics; let us therefore listen to him scrutinizing More's famous *Utopia* (his No Place and/or Good Place). In view of still widespread misinterpretation of More's attitude to the social practices of the Utopians – not to speak of his reasons for writing his book and of his views about human motivation – Augustine will have to set out his own interpretation of More's views of the 'good place' he has created.

More presents Utopia as a would-be perfect society organized on theoretically rational lines by a military despot. The idea of the perfect society harks back to Plato's *Republic*, but the mentality of the Utopians, apart from their enthusiasm for common possession of property, is fostered by a mixture of Stoicism – insofar as they strive for dutiful virtue – and a supposedly Epicurean hedonism combined with utilitarianism that sounds more like Mill's gentler and less philistine version than Bentham's cruder but more coherent original. Although the Utopians think that there are higher and lower pleasures, and that the higher pleasures of culture and virtue should be preferred, More's protagonist Raphael Hythlodaeus –

which name indicates someone who sees evil but talks nonsense about curing it – claims he is not defending Utopian practices, merely describing them, and that though they seem rational, they might be improved by an injection of revealed truth. (*CU* 178): this, he adds, seems obviously true in the case of pleasure, for he allows that without religious scruple Utopian hedonism would be more blatant. Even so, the Utopians fail to recognize that pleasure should be welcomed as a worthy concomitant of virtue rather than sought for its own sake.

A more basic weakness of Utopian rationality – and one that our Augustine will make explicit – is that their society is constructed on naturalistic lines. In contrast to what obtains in Plato's *Republic*, there is no metaphysical superstructure within which the destiny of man is worked out – despite the fact that the Utopians hold that disbelief in Providence (the disbelief taught by Epicurus himself and the more genuinely Epicurean among More's contemporaries) is a disgrace. With some metaphysical and effectively transcendent religious foundation, the Utopians would be less likely to make mistakes, not least about pleasure.

Utopian society is homogenized. They drink wine but apparently are not allowed beer. They have no private property. They dress alike and their activities, especially their sexual activities, are strictly monitored: in this respect they may seem (apart from the beer) to resemble the Carthusian monks in London whom More much admired, not to say the coming Geneva of Calvin! More, however, puts forward good Augustinian reasons for so ordering them; throughout the world human beings are small-minded, envious, violent, vengeful, driven by fear and hatred rather than love, too often dominated by a lust for power.

Much of this psychological analysis sounds Augustinian, and Utopian society is to be a rational rectification of such human weaknesses. More makes it clear that Hythlodaeus's criticism of existing Christian societies is justified in respect of their militarism, dishonesty, oppressive laws, parasitic courts and gross neglect of the poor. Yet the solutions developed in Utopia demand not only homogenization and denial of individuality – aims Augustine finds philosophically repellent – but a whole series of 'rational' practices generally contradicted or disowned by Christians. Wherever possible, they employ savage mercenaries to fight for them, having no concern about how many of these barbarians lose their lives; they encourage the assassination of foreign leaders and bribe would-be assassins; they are enthusiastic for suicide – albeit no one is compelled to take his own life – and in keeping with their hedonism and utilitarianism, their religion is idolatrous. The best that 'reason' can offer in regard to worship (taking both the cosmic and the political into account) is the cult of the heavenly bodies or of human benefactors, both of which Augustine had condemned in *The City of God*.

The Utopians allow a great deal of religious diversity. As we have seen, our Augustine will tolerate more of this than he once did; nonetheless, he will find their reasons for toleration unacceptable. Agreeing with his one-time pagan patron Symmachus, enemy of his later spiritual father Ambrose, and he of, 'it is not by one road that [we approach] so great a secret', they think that all religions provide an equally good way to salvation. That, in Augustine's view, is not only unchristian but also irrational in that it seems to imply that all life-choices are equally spiritual, disallowing legitimate criticism (let alone condemnation) of one religion by adherents of another.

Utopia, More indicates, has been constructed by those better at recognizing wrongs in an apparently Christian Europe than at offering a cure for them that does not look as bad as the malady. Nevertheless, it is more or less the best human ingenuity can come up with – and our Augustine – more strongly than More himself – will concentrate his criticism on a Utopian disregard for our uniqueness as individuals formed in the image of God, to which he had borne personal testimony in the *Confessions*. Indeed, he will criticize More himself on this score, who despite his hostility to the triviality of late medieval logic-chopping – in which his Utopians are happily not as well versed as 'we' are – has followed medieval Aristotelianism in underestimating the unique possibilities of each individual. Yet though More's view of the nature and lifestyle of the better sort of Christian is flawed, Augustine will applaud his recognition that Utopian attempts to 'remake' humanity generate a political manipulation governed by an irreducible hedonism – with or without a contempt for 'outsiders'; even of those who do what they are told. He will observe that the project of Utopus has disquieting similarities to those of Rousseau and Marx, not to mention Robespierre, Hitler and Mao.

Accordingly, our Augustine will find More, opponent of political panaceas and revolutionary moves in statecraft, upholder of a gradualist approach to political reform, to have combined an

Augustinian vision of human nature with a reasonably Augustinian account of how the Christian politician should proceed. Of course, even among those who accept Augustine's empirical account of man's nature, other options are open – which may produce yet another political panacea or its opposite: political life viewed as a wilderness that the clever man can tame in his own interest. Machiavelli is the example *par excellence* of the latter opinion, Hobbes one of the first of the former, though the cynically Hobbesian panacea is comparatively unambitious – even immediately harmless – since not tied to any historicist account of human progress (as were visions of Hegel, Marx and Heidegger, the totalitarian heirs of 1789). Our Augustine will ask us to look briefly at some of these thinkers in chronological order before returning to further reflection on the more contemporary democratic scene.

Machiavelli's *Prince* was composed (though not published) shortly before More's *Utopia*, and though More could not have read it, he was surely not unaware of some of its thinking; his rival, Thomas Cromwell, certainly knew of it, may have read it in some form, and accepted at least some significant features of the Italian story. He seems to have combined a genuine Protestantism (or at least anti-Romanism) with the belief that authority should reside solely in the hands of an absolute monarch, being in that, at least, a predecessor of Hobbes.

Political as well as theological anti-Romanism must be attributed to Machiavelli, convinced as he was of the harm the Roman Church had done to Italy – not least in keeping it divided and thus the prey of foreign powers – and in 'metaphysical' revolt against the older intellectual structures of Christendom and their associated moral principles. Philosophically he was a genuine Epicurean – not a woolly minded one like those of his contemporaries who tried to combine Epicureanism with a belief in a Christian Providence. He owned a much-loved and annotated copy of the newly rediscovered poem of the Roman Lucretius – *On the Nature of Things* – and found in its Epicurean cosmic indeterminism a likely explanation both of the freedom of the human will and of the apparently arbitrary character of both cosmic and human activity.

The man of virtue (*virtù*), Machiavelli believed, is best able to handle the contingencies that ever befall human affairs, whether in civil or ecclesiastical politics. Cesare Borgia was exceptionally skilled in this regard, yet in the end he too failed fatally by neglecting

to factor in that at the time of his papal father's death he too would
be gravely ill. Yet Machiavelli – like many in the Middle Ages –
largely agrees with Augustine (and More) about the radically
envious character of a vengeful human nature, driven by fear rather
than love, and, he adds, in the 'better' sort by the desire to be free to
dominate others. He has, however, abandoned the traditional and
Augustinian view that to be free means to desire only the good in
favour of the more modern account of it as the liberty to do what
one likes. Most people, he believes, want merely to be free from
the interference of others, while the 'virtuous' want freedom to
dominate others: in both cases the sense of a common good, of man
as a social animal, has disappeared, and the way is open (though
Machiavelli prefers to go elsewhere) to view political and social
structures not as natural growths but as the result of deals between
'free' individuals to protect themselves against other 'free' persons.

Like Machiavelli, Hobbes longed for peace, not, as the Italian, by
clearing the 'barbarians' (that is, chiefly the French) out of Italy, but
by ending the disastrous civil wars of religion. That – and other means
to survival – can only be achieved under a despotism with the despot
allowed to rule unmolested if and only if he can ensure our survival;
if not, he shall be rightly deposed and replaced by a more effective
master. Reflecting on such a solution our Augustine will again see
the cure as worse than the illness, for although Hobbes will quote
the Scriptures endlessly – and whether or not there is reason to think
of him as a crypto-atheist – he would be the last to allow religious
scruples to stand in the way of necessarily absolute sovereign rule.
In the Middle Ages, our Augustine will remind him, the doctrine of
the two swords (ascribed to himself) at least allowed Catholics the
freedom to practise their religion without fear, indeed to proselytize
when the opportunity arose. That, he will realize, would be the
last thing Hobbes has in mind: any religion which (like Catholic
Christianity) sought to establish its rights to conscience against the
State, would be undermining the State's sovereign foundations.

Augustine will reply that the abolition of the right to practise and
to preach Catholic Christianity indicates the theophobic nature of
Hobbesian society, and would only invite the Christian to defy the
law, as would nothing else. And he would be right, since believing
man is created in the image and likeness of God, while Hobbes –
concerned only with how he can survive, preferably with a degree
of comfort – views despotism as the only panacea against sectarian

warfare and persecution, with Catholic Christianity by definition a non-reformable troublemaker.

Hobbes is willing to pay a high price to save his skin and ours – concluding there is no other way. Nevertheless, from Augustine's point of view, though important historically, he is a comparatively minor offender against God and man. He does not attempt to reconstruct man in some para-godlike image. Though authoritarian, and thus from Augustine's point of view reprehensible, and though believing his doctrines are to be instilled *via* universities, he is no full-blooded totalitarian. To reach that end-state we await the eighteenth-century French Enlightenment, especially in the person of Rousseau: origin, wittingly or not, of both the police State and of intolerant self-styled 'liberal' variations on it.

For Rousseau, who unlike Hobbes claimed to be a specifically *moral* – even at times a Christian – reformer, man is corrupted *by* society; *pace* Augustine there is no genetic weakness, no 'original sin' haunting the human race. European society, bourgeois and hypocritical, offers the finest witness to what has gone wrong. Even Rousseau's own misdemeanours – lying about a maidservant and thus ensuring her resort to prostitution when she consequentially lost her position, the abandonment of his illegitimate children in various orphanages – are no fault of their perpetrator but of the wicked society from which he himself has not escaped unscathed. The cure is the right kind of (Hobbesian) education; this Rousseau holds should be regularly taught and even preached (as already in *Leviathan* 30.14): an education our Augustine will identify as brainwashing, observing that while he himself had written his *Confessions* to praise God and ask for his pardon, Rousseau had emulated and parodied him by writing confessions that are little more than a long and elegant series of self-justifications.

Rousseau claimed – disingenuously or naively – that the proper 'education' should not be imposed by order of the State. Many, however, soon saw that as the best way to achieve it. Here again Rousseau (or at least his successors) show themselves more 'modern' than Hobbes who appears still to live in the ancient world where even Plato's nihilist Thrasymachus of the *Republic* distinguishes between public and private life, only the former being the world of power-politics. Those (such as obviously all females) who live only in the private world are more or less safe from the immediate interference or manipulation of the State. For male citizens so to live would be wimpish.

With Oliver Cromwell's execution of King Charles and his subsequent 'puritanical' rule through major-generals, things had already moved in a more 'modern' direction. In the French Revolution of 1789 the pace of change increased dramatically: we have total mobilization, total State control, total war; the perfected 'totalitarian' State is born: the State of Hitler, Stalin, Mao and many lesser imitators. From our Augustine's point of view, things are worse than anything he might have imagined in his own day, since even the private life of the citizens is now under State control. He recalls that before the conversion of Constantine, Christians were on the whole happy to remain a quiet sect without interest in politics or in a public life; that they willingly left to pagans. Only the pagans' fear that this opting-out was in fact dangerous – that the gods might not like it – rendered their quietism insecure, and raised the cry: 'Christians to the lion'.

Nor is it just total control that our Augustine will find offensive; but total control for an evil end, that is, to remake the human race. 'These things shall be; a loftier race/than ere the world hath known shall rise,' as an Anglican imperial hymn so succinctly puts it. That loftier race, far from moulded in the image and likeness of God, is proclaimed as the coming of some supposed necessity: it may be the biological destiny of the 'Aryans', or a predetermined society identified according to the axioms of an Economic Determinism recognized by the 'scientific' observations of new (and always anti-Christian) prophets. Our Augustine will tell us that with the baptized and reborn Christian replaced by the New Storm Trooper, by Soviet Man, or some other variant of the same theme, divine predestination – God's preparation of good for his elect – has mutated into a materialist and immanent determinism from which God is necessarily excluded.

While Augustine's strictures on post-Rousseau totalitarian régimes will hardly surprise us, such comments on liberal democracy – some of which he has recorded in the previous chapter – will be hardly less severe at the theoretical level, even while he will realize that the more obviously totalitarian options are in the short term more lethal. Augustine's criticisms of our own favourite political system will continue to be sharp, and he will trace back its current misfortunes to the radical dechristianization of Europe that began following the disasters of the seventeenth century wars of religion, reaching its theoretical – but not yet its practical – climax with the Enlightenment. Not that he will argue that nothing good came out of that movement: ironically, he will recall that it has enabled us to develop a biblical scholarship that avoids a long-standing theological and philosophical embarrassment about a number of texts (especially from the Old Testament) which the anti-Christians of the Enlightenment latched on to as depicting the Christian God as a primitive and barbarian deity.

Our Augustine will inspect five basic principles of liberalism (and/or liberal democracy), simple or complex, to indicate how they are far from offering a panacea for our political ills.

1   We are all possessed of natural rights, but these appear to be viewed as quasi-metaphysical entities; thus, contemporary defences of them must be substantially different from those proposed by early modern thinkers such as Locke or Grotius. Augustine will again defer discussion of rights, merely noting that they raise a host of questions: How do we know what rights we have, if any? By what standard are we to resolve situations where rights-claims seem to collide? What metaphysical deductions must follow from any claim that human rights are inalienable?

2   Since in a 'liberal' society there can be no metaphysical foundation for inalienable rights, they are sometimes stipulated and established by appeal to social contract. Not least of the problems with that is that social contracts are fictions – little more than reifications of our being born inevitably into some particular society! Or they depend on some hypothetical state of nature; but if that state is no paradise, such as Hobbes well knew it could not be, it remains a mere construct of those who happen to find it useful: hardly a compelling reason for accepting it as the foundation for moral obligations. The same applies to hypothetically rational conditions, such as those envisaged by John Rawls behind his 'veil of ignorance'. Augustine has already noted that in that scenario individuals are not reasoning in human circumstances, indeed can hardly recognize themselves as actual human beings.

There are two kinds of contract invoked in accounts of liberalism: one based on prudence, the other on some supposedly moral foundation. Our Augustine will object to the latter on the ground that it precisely *lacks* defensible foundation – as many of its advocates are obliged to admit – apart, that is, from something theistic that they are not prepared to accept. While he will allow that prudential contracts are more defensible, he will observe that they afford no adequate protection for those unable to make, or even assent to and accept, the contract: not only the unborn, but young children, those suffering from mental illnesses and the senile. He will point out that the increasing violence directed or advocated against such groups is morally unacceptable, yet derives from the nature of the supposed contract itself. He predicts that contractarians of this ilk will advocate (and eventually achieve) widespread acceptance of abortion, infanticide and elimination of the debilitated by euthanasia.

3   Some liberals will appeal to a strong form of consequentialism; again Augustine will defer detailed comment, contenting himself for the moment with reminding us that consequentialisms vary with what are recognized as *good* consequences, and that almost all modern consequentialisms offer a materialist, if not philistine, account of what goods humanity – or rather individual humans – do best to pursue.

4   Underlying many of the ill-defended claims already listed, Augustine will point to a number of conceptual errors: first that we are (or are assumed to be) atomic and deracinated individuals – whereas we are naturally social and cannot develop as we should outside the family and outside society – nor merely by 'deals' within it. Societies are natural (though they all are to a degree perverse) and though individuals are prior to society (in that a society's value depends on what it can offer an individual), a good enough society is a necessary condition for individual growth. Augustine will insist that within society the family be the matrix of procreation: the generation of children cannot be allowed to fall into the clutches of a public authority that would eliminate the authority of parents in favour of its own, thus promoting surrogacy, in vitro

fertilization and other devices to bypass the need for what it supplants.

Thus our Augustine will hold that the nearer a society to the morality, even if rarely actualized, of the Catholic Church, the greater will be the chances for the human and spiritual growth of the persons who compose it. Hence societies are of unequal value, and though a certain toleration of error is necessary if we are to accept that human dignity implies a God-given freedom of the will to act or to fail to act well, toleration is no intrinsic good and certain evil forms of society – secular or religious – should be opposed, restrained and if necessary suppressed.

5   Finally, Augustine will argue that whereas in 'liberal' societies impersonal justice trumps claims about goodness, yet if justice *is* a good, then it itself depends on that goodness it improperly claims to trump! Impersonal justice, in calling for nothing more than judicial equality, points to a society in which third-person and impersonal claims are always to outweigh those of more local loyalties: thus there would be no reason why I should choose to defend my child in preference to a stranger's if such a dreadful choice were to confront me.

Consequently, our Augustine will have no time for any form of egalitarianism except that which holds that we all are of equal – equally high – value insofar as we are created in the image of God. That does not imply that all our choices – for example, of lifestyles – are equally to be respected (or even necessarily tolerated); nor, as we would all (if honest) admit, that there are no essential differences in our abilities, be it in the arts, the sciences, the capacity to govern or to teach. Augustine will agree with Nietzsche that a liberal society risks either degenerating into populism, or will be driven by envy and a radical hostility to any kind of authority. Or it will idolize a mediocrity dressed up as egalitarian: with friendship a mere cronyism, the kind of companionship in crime of the young Augustine who, as one of the 'boys', would boast of more unchastity than he really knew, and rejoice in wickedness just because it is wicked – as the futile destruction of someone's crop of pears (C, 2.3.7; 2.8.16). We might compare the contemporary lout who idly scratches cars!

Our Augustine will know that in the early modern period we largely abandoned final causation in physics, and that this proved to be advantageous for immediate scientific progress, but that increasingly since then, idolizing the so-called Enlightenment, we have also abandoned final causes in ethics – and so an over-arching goodness – for which we have paid a terrible price. Along with that, we have preferred to banish Original Sin, rashly supposing human evil can be cured by a 'progressive' education: we have forgotten that to learn to reason is also to learn to rationalize our wicked desires (like Rousseau, our patron saint, and Adam and Eve our forebears); that there is no evidence for our assumption that more 'educated' individuals are better citizens than their uneducated fellows: that indeed the opposite is often the case.

Nor has Augustine finished there. In losing sight of God and the Christian theory of man as created in God's image, we have come to believe that curing social defects is simply a matter of passing new and supposedly enlightened laws, forgetting that laws, though they can be helpful in teaching or inducing habits of morality, can only inculcate them incompletely and – being man-made – can easily be – and are – reversed. Eventually – since we are now supposed to be atomic individuals who know that 'common good' is a mere euphemism for the target of selfishly fuelled deals for our profit – we can expect to be abandoned as worthless parasites when we no longer bring the desired profit to the deal-maker's table.

Insofar as it presents itself as a panacea, our Augustine will bracket our liberal democracy with totalitarian régimes – for in a panacea no variations are to be tolerated. Hence, he will note, liberal-democratic States are regularly hostile to religion in general but to the Christian religion in particular, since rightly understanding it offers a very different view of the nature and goals of humanity. For Christians, as he will continue to urge repeatedly, man derives his worth from his or her being created in God's image; hence his or her worth is intrinsic. For liberal democrats, we are supposed to be equal, but that equality, far from being metaphysically based, rests on the sense (as Hobbes understood) of being the safest delusion for us all: that since as atomic individuals we know that we cannot go it alone, we must be recognized by others as able to contribute; if not, we are to be thrown on the scrap heap – and what else should we expect, Augustine will conclude, when the 'scientific' value of the individual is zero: that 'scientific' sense in which we are all equal.

And it is to obviate this all too evident conclusion, Augustine will notice, that some now propose a 'virtual' morality: though we know we have no value, let us claim that we have, and let us discourage people from asking whether such a claim can be justified. Hence our Augustine's most basic and most challenging charge against liberal democracy will be that (like more obviously totalitarian systems) it relies on fraud and deception; hence can be expected to become exponentially corrupt – not that the value judgement can have any intrinsic meaning – and the further it retreats from its Christian roots, the more 'corrupt' it will become. So much, hence, for hopes resting on this panacea.

Our Augustine will have a final question: in our liberal-democratic world, who are the wise counsellors, those to whom we should look for moral advice? In the past, they have been priests or other venerable figures – not least bishops like himself. Now he is distressed, though hardly surprised, to find things very different: priests (if still exuding a whiff of the transcendent) are largely ignored if not maligned, while, and despite our egalitarian principles, technical experts and psychologists may be rated highly. However, since our worship of secular expertise runs in parallel with the egalitarian principle that we are all as wise and good as one another – all must receive prizes and the same high marks individually and culturally – fame rather than expertise as promoted through the electronic media will be the fall-back guide for the ill-informed and half-educated populace. The bishop will be replaced by, for instance, the pop star, the soccer player and the reality-show 'actress'. Augustine may be especially surprised (until he recalls his own theories of Original Sin) if he eventually finds a pope who, if he is to be an oracle, may be drawn into the style of a 'celeb'.

6

Utilitarians and Kantians: A Parallel Journey to Triviality?

It is good that one man die for the people.

CAIAPHAS

Augustine Redivivus will come across the word 'consequentialist' almost every time he looks into a book about moral philosophy: sometimes as a word of praise, sometimes of reprobation. When he first enquired what the word meant, he was puzzled to hear that consequentialists are 'teleologists', in that they judge the morality of actions (whether more or less exclusively) by their recognized or intended results. Thus he hears that some of them – a subgroup calling themselves 'utilitarians' – say moral acts are those which (whether individually or as a type) promote 'the greatest good of the greatest number'. He found that puzzling: as he hears others pointing out, it seems impossible to do the 'calculus' required to know whether act A or act B contributes more to the happiness of the greatest number. In any case (as a man from Christian antiquity) he failed to see how such calculations, even if possible, could contribute to the happiness of the human *individual*; he still is committed to assuming morality intrinsically connected with being happy and hence that different moral systems depend on differing assumptions as to what counts as happiness. He was also concerned because, if the end-result is all that matters, what conclusions are to be drawn about the *responsibility* of each individual to live virtuously, regardless of whether his virtuous acts are (or could be) effective?

Augustine believes that the virtuous man is happy – or at least as happy as anyone can be in the present life – but fails to see how his desired virtue can depend exclusively on results immediately achieved, either for himself or for others, or indeed for humanity in general. He recognizes that results are important, in that it would be immoral to seek for anything other than what seems the best possible outcome all things considered, even if that outcome is unachievable, but he still clings to the belief that the disposition he has when he does his best is important. He thinks it better, for example, to help an old lady cross the road simply because that is a good thing to do, than in the hope that he will benefit in her will (even if he has an idea that he might). Therefore, he seeks further contemporary enlightenment.

He begins by noting some comments made by consequentialists: that the agent's virtue is part of the good to be achieved; or that consequentialism need not (though often does) imply that the end justifies the means – whatever they may be. For the means should not contradict the ends. Thus he may be told that holding an election is a good means of securing a democracy, but that if that election is intended to promote those who intend that under their elected rule there will be no further elections, then such an election is only apparently democratic, being the means to secure an undemocratic end.

Our Augustine remains dissatisfied: he wants to know what kind of thing this 'democracy' is, in theory and in reality, and whether it promotes the good of those who act or are acted upon according to its rules. Indeed, he wants to understand how we can determine good ends if we do not know what is good for the individual or for society.

He is now told the history of utilitarianism, which he realizes, may also be relevant to other forms of consequentialism. Although he cannot recall people called utilitarians in his own earlier society, he notes that some sort of consequentialism had been advocated by a man he particularly disliked – albeit he now knows that 'beast' was often depicted as 'worse' than he really was. That man was Epicurus, and Augustine remembers that he had read a saying of Epicurus to the effect that he spat on virtue unless it brought him pleasure; in the twenty-first century he wonders whether virtue would not suffer similarly at the hands of our latter-day consequentialists.

Augustine's unease will have grown greater on learning that Jeremy Bentham, founder of the modern utilitarian school, resembles Epicurus in holding that the good is pleasure, though measured in an apparently scientific way. Bentham supposed it could be measured in units, not, as Epicurus more modestly held, that it is somehow to be identified as a mere absence of pain or distress. Yet even apart from the difficulty our Augustine feels about measuring those units, he wonders whether pleasures of the soul can be subject to the same measuring strategies as physical pleasures. Does following Bentham imply that all pleasures are of the senses? How does one measure the pleasures of the mind, such as those of mathematics, or of the worship of a beneficent Deity? Perhaps to be a consequentialist entails or should entail being an atheist: an odd-seeming reason to be an atheist; perhaps rather a reason against being a consequentialist!

Augustine will find scant in common with Bentham, but will observe that, officially at least, Bentham's version of utilitarianism is recently little followed, though one of its more apparently self-contradictory characteristics – which Epicurus would have regarded as resulting from a perverse error of judgement – retains some popularity. Unlike Epicureans, modern consequentialists, utilitarians included, must seem to be philanthropic in the sense of purporting to love the human race. Though Epicurus might accept the logic of Bentham's dictum that natural rights are 'nonsense upon stilts' – as, Augustine would agree, they must be in a non-providentialist world – even he would remain uneasy about Bentham's explanation of his philanthropic activities. 'I just like doing that sort of thing' he is reputed to have said – and it does not need an Augustine to point out that others 'just like' very different and more sinister pursuits. Augustine agrees that on this point Epicurus, whose frequently cited motto was 'Live avoiding notice' (Usener, *Epicurea*, section 551), is more coherent (albeit that coherence earned its author a reputation as monstrously antisocial).

Within the utilitarian tradition itself, as Augustine will learn, there had been a reaction against Bentham's philistine account of pleasure and his apparently subhuman view of the good life for mankind. He hears how Bentham's associate James Mill had subjected his son to an educational régime on utilitarian lines that had produced a nervous breakdown, and that the son recognized the 'education' he had received as part of the problem. So Augustine was interested in how John Stuart, the younger Mill, reacting to this debacle, discovered he had been influenced by non-utilitarian sources even when still victim of his father's educational shibboleths.

Mill, so Augustine learns, had respected the poet Coleridge, who knew something about Kant and had picked up a curious variety of Platonism – better Neoplatonism – in Germany. And Mill was prepared to countenance Auguste Comte's crazy version of a 'religion of humanity', though eventually, with some regret, he dismissed it as the project of a man who had never managed to laugh: a strange comment from someone who seems scarcely to have been able to laugh himself.

Augustine discovered that Mill – partly through Coleridge – had learned some disconcerting ideas, whether from Plato or from such other Platonists or would-be Platonists as he knew or read of: ideas of a kind almost to lift him to metaphysics. Though he managed to resist that, he was unable to resist the conclusion that the pleasures of pigs are inadequate for human beings and famously to pronounce Socrates dissatisfied better than a pig satisfied. Augustine saw the point: who, he mused, would want to eat like a pig! Perhaps even a dissatisfied Socrates would contribute to the greater good of the greatest number.

Our Augustine will have a certain sympathy (though not much) with Mill's apparent Platonism, as at least a move in the right direction. He is eager to see how this search for 'higher' values might dilute the utilitarianism that had done the young John Stuart so much harm, only to realize that, far from solving the clash between the two traditions, Mill had tried to cling to both, pleasing neither the Platonists nor those more consistent utilitarians who reject his newfangled (or rather outdated) emphasis on more 'intellectual' – even 'spiritual' – virtues as incompatible with the search for that elusive greatest good of the greatest number. The search for an abstract good of 'humanity' is hard to square with making oneself individually a better person.

Augustine, as he reads on in this strange history, will hardly be surprised by its conclusion. For allowing that Bentham's account of the good seemed unworthy and finding Mill's attempt to blend Bentham with some sort of qualitative evaluation of pleasures normally accounted a failure, some later utilitarians resorted to G. E. Moore's notion of the good as an undefinable non-natural quality, albeit to justify that requires a heftier dose of metaphysics than Moore accounted credible. Yet Virginia Woolf and her Bloomsbury set hailed his conclusion, however incoherent, as a huge advance on the crudely revised Benthamism of Henry Sidgwick.

Giving up on Moore's apparent lurch towards metaphysics, later members of the utilitarian sect had moved to proclaiming that we should maximize the good for the human race, whatever that good happens to be. Which means that unless we can determine the nature of the good – Augustine will observe that though Plato made some real progress on this, we, or at least many of our professionals, have largely forgotten or ignored it – then utilitarianism, as indeed any other form of consequentialism, reduces itself to 'preference theory': the good is what we 'prefer', or – quite nakedly – 'want'.

That does not mean that it is useless. Augustine, working from the exemplar he gave long ago that Vespasian was a better emperor than Domitian (CG, 5.21), will agree that some people's preferences are objectively better – prudentially if not morally – than others, but he will add that to stop there is little better than whistling in the wind. Utilitarians may offer prudential reasons – which they may prefer to call moral reasons – for preferring one action to another, yet provide no indication of how to posit plausible, let alone intelligible, foundations for universally binding norms that can hope to command general assent.

Augustine's fundamental objection to any overriding consequentialism is that it can provide no account of the good as a measure for individual preferences. Of course, if God – or the right kind of God – exists, things will look rather different. However, that 'right kind of God' is important. In ancient Hippo, Augustine had rejected the God (or One) of Plotinus precisely because he (or it) is too abstract, too unconcerned with human affairs, too unfitted to act as a mediator and supporter of human beings: in brief because that type of 'goodness' is not good enough.

Disillusioned, our Augustine will return to the history of utilitarianism, and conclude that since utilitarians can give no coherent account of what is good, either for individuals or for society, their principle that we must judge by the results of what we do is of no practical use – unless, that is, we are prepared to accept that the good for us, individually and collectively, is nothing more than what we prefer to achieve (in ignorance of our life experiences and their import). He will then spot that a similarly reductive regression to a mere formalism dogs other varieties of contemporary thinking, not least the theories of those who consider themselves, to greater or lesser degree, followers of Kant.

The history of Kantianism, our Augustine will argue, runs parallel to that of the utilitarians, except that it introduces into the heart of its moral claims a thesis that seems peculiarly perverse: a claim to human autonomy about which he has already complained, but which is now, he finds, widely assumed to be both possible and desirable. Not, he realizes, that Kant was the first to introduce it – its origins go back via Locke and the Cambridge Platonists to the Renaissance, if not earlier – but the form in which he finds it most influentially advanced has been developed by Kant, though now defended – if at all, for it is more often than not an undefended axiom – very differently.

Augustine knows that in the age of faith we call the Middle Ages such a theory could not be formulated. Then all taught (though, as ever, few lived in accordance with what they taught) that man is created by God and lives in a world, including a moral world, that God has decreed, while moral values depend not only on his 'will' (as many but not all of them saw it) but more fundamentally on his nature. Augustine also knows that in the ancient world, Kantian notions of human autonomy were rejected not only by Christians, but in influential cases – and commonly at least to a degree – by pagans: not least by Plotinus, the pagan whose metaphysics he particularly admired. For Plotinus tells us that we have been deluded by pleasure, and by a desire to be self-creators (*Ennead* 5.1.1, as Kantians should note) into 'forgetting' our 'father', the supreme metaphysical being who is the source of our existence and our nature, including our moral capacities. Although Plotinus holds the typically Platonic but non-Christian view that we are 'naturally' immortal, he nevertheless believes that that natural state depends on the existence and causative power of the 'father'. Autonomy, Kantian or other, on such a scenario is a delusion.

Autonomy in Kant has many sources, two of which are Christian: the desire (if problematically explained) to allow fallen human beings enough 'free' will to be held responsible for their actions; then the claim that all human beings are in some sense equal: that is, insofar as all are created in the image and likeness of

God. By Kant's time that religious claim had been given its more sinister and secular interpretation by Rousseau: all men are equal *democratically* – which means that if we know what it is to be democratic – and the General Will informs us as to that – we know the kind of secular equality we all have. Kant, therefore, believes he is justified in claiming that we are uniquely valuable as human individuals, and that this equality is manifested in an equal moral capacity.

That suggestion, our Augustine will maintain, is very implausible – even leaving aside the effects of our particular environment and our individual genetic history. Kant, however, tried to prop up his thesis with an impossible account of what it is to be human, as Augustine will have noted: a theory which divides us into our 'noumenal' and 'phenomenal' selves, insisting that the 'noumenal' self is the real 'we'. Thus, we are equal as rational agents, but *that* claim depends on two further implausible axioms: that rationality can supply us with moral obligations (*pace* Hume), and that we are – more dualistically – not bodily, but solely spiritual and rational beings.

Augustine had already met and dismissed that idea in Porphyry, the disciple of Plotinus who held that 'we should flee everything bodily' (*omne corpus est fugiendum*: R, 1.4.3). He continues to condemn it not only as non-Christian but as empirically absurd, even though he recalls that it attracted him in his younger days – indeed that even in later life he could not explain how we are embodied souls, but had and has every reason to believe that that is what we are.

Pushing on with his study of the Kantian tradition, as previously the utilitarian, our Augustine soon finds in the twenty-first century people, calling themselves constructivists, who claim to present Kant reformed. Like their master they insist that we are autonomous, hence must prescribe rational rules to ourselves of a sort such that we would all accept – for others as for ourselves – if we were set 'behind a veil of ignorance', thus remaining purely 'noumenal' (as Kant put it) or at least rational beings. Augustine, however, has already observed that there is no reason why we humans should do whatever a being devoid of any personal history would do when set behind a veil. In his *City of God* and elsewhere he had argued, against the abstractions of the Neoplatonists, that it is our personal history that makes us what we are, within the broad parameters of being human. Nor, he will add once more, could we as humans ever be in a position unerringly to know the right and rational course in all relevant circumstances, let alone be able to follow it.

As he will later explain, returning to a theme he has already deemed highly significant, Augustine is much concerned with those situations, common enough in our lives, in which we know we shall regret whatever course of action we shall choose, yet have no option but to choose one of them, even if by default. He has treated of regret already, he continues, so we can leave it on one side, only recognizing that when we try to prescribe rational rules for ourselves, we find no agreement as to the nature of the good underlying the right choices that we are trying to make, so in effect fall back on what we believe (or prefer to believe) to be the good to which justice points. With Kantians, as with utilitarians, Augustine will recognize high-minded claims collapsing into preference theories, and ultimately into the apotheosis of Choice.

There is worse to come: if we set ourselves up as able to decide by choice what is good and what is rational, we thereby lay claim to an autonomy denied by one of Augustine's basic beliefs: that we are not autonomous, but dependent. If there is a good, therefore, we need it but *cannot* construct it; we must *discover* it. In the fifth century Augustine, fighting what we now dub Pelagianism, could have formulated the axiom that 'ought does not entail can': in theological terms 'ought' implies my being able to do what I ought with and only with God's help. Again, Augustine will cite Robert Browning's *Abt Vogler* about a man's reach being 'beyond his grasp – or what's a heaven for?' For good measure he will add that 'heaven' is a theological concept and used abusively or at best metaphorically outside a properly theological context. Pelagians, whether in an ancient or more modern 'constructivist' and 'Kantian' guise, simply are wrong to claim that we can do what we ought to do – and that will often be true even if we 'construct' what we ought to do.

In sum, Kantians – as consequentialists, utilitarian or other – claim, covertly or openly, to know both what is good and that they are capable of achieving what they choose to hold good. Yet if ignorance is the guide to the good we construct, then claims to autonomy – to be self-makers insofar as we invent the moral universe – or even more widely if we note the more recent more 'post-humanist' versions of self-creation – reveal themselves as radically incoherent. Even if they were plausible, there is no logical reason why autonomy would bring happiness, let alone an adequate sense of duty.

Our Augustine approves of Sidgwick's admission at the end of his 500-page *Methods of Ethics* of his failure to show how duty can be compatible with happiness: a Kantian project set within a utilitarian frame. He believes both that we cannot avoid pursuing happiness – however misguidedly we go about it – and that unless we have some better guide to the good which will bring it about, we shall never find it. 'Our heart is restless until it rests in Thee' (C, 1.1.1), he will murmur again, recalling how near the end of his life he wrote about his *Confessions* that he would hardly want to change a word of it!

And our Augustine will go further. Much modern ethical discussion, he will conclude, is in purely formal mode: pursue the good – whatever it may be. He will add that in the absence of God or at least some entity viewed as transcendental – such as a Platonic Form or the Plotinian One – so disappointingly uninformative a conclusion is both inevitable and of virtually no practical use. So how does he find the current generation of ethicists reacting to that situation? Some, he will note, like the late Richard Rorty, may decide that there is no future in philosophy (nor *a fortiori* in theology) and seek their fortunes elsewhere: Rorty himself resorted to a department of Comparative Literature, where you could spot disturbing human situations well or badly recorded or imagined, without the necessity of evaluating the truth or falsehood of the ethical dilemmas they evoke.

Falling back on formalism, or giving up on moral philosophy in favour of deals to survive in a multicultural democracy where it is taboo to account any one ethical theory better than another, will never satisfy the ordinary man or woman who may not think very hard, but yet believes that there is difference between right and wrong – even though he or she lacks the tools to understand how that difference might be intelligibly expressed. To overcome this obstacle, a newly fashionable philosophical approach has been laid on the table; one Augustine must detest since it commits the philosopher to deliberate deception.

In any society, there is a gap between intellectual élites – who may also more or less overlap with the governing élites – and the ordinary public. Augustine will recognize that in the twenty-first century that gap has in many respects widened on a scale perhaps hitherto unknown. Many Western élites have no moral principles, relying largely on prudential considerations to satisfy their needs (and it may be the needs of others); but they fear social upheaval if having no principles were to become fashionable with the man-in-the-street – as Sidgwick wrote when concluding *Methods of Ethics*: I have failed, but it would be a social catastrophe if my failure to reconcile duty and happiness were to become widely known; therefore we must deceive, if not lie.

Augustine is very severe about lying, believing that it is never permissible – a view he might now want slightly to modify – but be that as it may, he assuredly will consider deliberate deception of the public (as indeed of themselves) by such philosophical élites as downright despicable. Nevertheless, he finds 'virtual morality' common currency: 'We, the enlightened, know the truth about so called morality; there is no such thing, but we must preserve this notion as a needful device to survive in the feared jungle of a value-free universe.' The historical Augustine had not read Plato's *Republic*, but by now will have corrected that gap in his education (enhancing his Greek as well as learning English) and so will be aware of Thrasymachus's claim that although we live in a value-free universe, people's naïve delusions about objective morality can be exploited in the rightly self-seeking interest of those smarter and 'stronger' (*Republic* 1, 338b, 348d).

Though our contemporary élites may agree with Thrasymachus at the theoretical level, they often prefer to hang what they propose for public consumption on something apparently higher-minded: the preservation of society, or even of the human race. Thus, although *we* 'know' that we have no free will but most people believe we have, it is expedient to encourage them in their error; or again, though the traditional virtues cannot be defended, we can talk about them as though they exist – perhaps even appear saviours of society in so doing. Our Augustine will not be impressed: a society protected by deception cannot be a good society, nor can those who propose such solutions deserve the honourable name of philosopher. Least of all should we deceive and be deceived in matters of religion and the value of religious systems. That, however, must await a later chapter.

Nevertheless, although he has no time for lying as social glue, Augustine is himself a consequentialist up to a point: far more so than many of his admirers want to admit; more especially those who apparently view the anti-consequentialist as committed to forgetting the importance of prudence and of serious thought about the unintended as well as the intended effects of behaviour. Results do matter, even if they have nothing to do with the immediate pursuit of virtue. As we have seen, Augustine held soldiers and executioners (better: prison guards) necessary – and would still find no reason not to hold them necessary – because the effects they produce are otherwise not possible. If they were, their services could be dispensed with and our regret over the 'collateral' consequences of their activities thus reduced. But since they are needed, we realize – as did Augustine then and will still now – the awesome consequences of living in a 'fallen' and 'penal' condition rather than amid such mere banalities as a value-free world can offer us.

7

Rights-Theory

In fourth- and fifth-century North Africa, Augustine had heard much philosophical discussion (and read much more), but would have heard little about rights or human rights. Now he finds rights regularly claimed (among others) by groups which regard themselves as persecuted subgroups, or as in some way victims of discrimination: thus racial minorities, women or homosexuals may now claim to be deprived of their rights. Such complaints (or at least complaints expressed in such terms) were unknown in Augustine's ancient world.

Of course, disputes conceptually related to modern rights-theory arose from time to time, as when in a Greek city-state 'democrats' might claim that all adult males should share the privileges of citizenship, or at least that all adult males should have some say in the government and in the administration of the laws. These 'rights' were seen as the privileges of a group like 'the people' and of agents acting in accordance with an objective justice. Claims about them seem far from the contemporary debate about subjective rights – not least if we think about the situation obtaining in city-states where 'the people' obtained power. There was no 'right' of appeal against their 'people's courts' (as Socrates discovered to his cost), and democracy meant the dictatorship of the majority (or of those who could control and thus claim to represent the majority). The notion of appeal courts would have been dismissed as undemocratic, while unlike in our own society, criminals were thought to have forfeited anything remotely a 'right', while foreigners never possessed them, being dependent on the good offices of a citizen-protector.

The situation in Western countries, and non-Western countries where Western influences have become strong, is now quite different: we hear constantly of human rights or of human rights abuses, and we know of political philosophers who claim that in moral and political debate 'rights are trumps'. Confronted with such a change, our Augustine is at first puzzled, and will want to investigate the question of rights further, under two main heads: historical and philosophical. He will want to know why rights have become so important, what happens when supposed rights clash, and more fundamentally, what a right is – which may seem a metaphysical question, not least if rights are to be granted the importance that those who hold that they are trumps – and indeed many less radical – want to maintain.

Subjective rights, that is, roughly, individual rights, were neither claimed nor recognized in the ancient world, nor for the most part in the Middle Ages. The rights of groups, however, became increasingly prominent: thus Magna Carta recognized certain rights of the clergy and the barons against the king, and more generally popes, kings, emperors and guilds all claimed rights for themselves against one another. One of the more important political debates of the medieval period was the so-called Investiture Contest whereby the Church claimed to have jurisdiction over its own, thus denying the Crown the responsibility of meting out justice to clergy. (In Oxford one such dispute – over the hanging of a clerical rapist by the civil authorities – is said to have led to the foundation of the University of Cambridge by a group of clerical refugees!) Yet although we might have expected that group rights would lead to the pursuit of individual rights, there is little medieval development along those lines. That is perhaps partly to be explained by the fact that even Christian salvation was thought of much more as a group aspiration, the salvation – that is, of the 'New Israel' – than it later became, especially under the influence of Protestantism.

Yet there were signs of the future from time to time. In the Peasants Revolt against King Richard II of England was heard for the first time the questioning slogan to be widely taken up in the seventeenth century during the turbulent period of the English Revolution: 'When Adam delved and Eve span, who was then the gentleman?' Here was an assertion of the rights of the individual against *both* the long-recognized competing parties, Church and State, albeit both in the main still regarded as natural growths and not, as later, rather as human constructs. In the seventeenth century, such slogans acquired the support of moral philosophers such as Grotius and Locke.

Our Augustine will recognize that these developments had a good side and a bad side. The good side would be that individual rights – especially in their Protestant version – were based on the claim that human beings are created in the image and likeness of God. The bad side would be that insofar as rights-claims were claims *against* authoritative institutions, they might, in the future, be claimed also *against* God's till then assumed highest and unchallengeable authority.

Both Grotius and Locke – and many of their immediate successors in what was still a uniformly Christian world – supposed that God distributes rights: that they are, in fact, the very expression of man's image-of-God status. God has granted all of us an equal chance of salvation combined with a human dignity that points to our spiritual independence from everything apart from Himself. Thus rights-theory, individualism and an individual-emphasizing version of Christianity can all be perceived as assertions of rights against both Church and State. Individual rights, that is, were an inference from Christian belief – and not least from the still strong theological currents pointing to a 'voluntarist' account of God's nature, works and overriding Will.

Does it follow from this, our Augustine will wonder, that societies which have no divine-image theory of man, or have abandoned it, lack justification for allowing subjective natural rights? That would have been the view both of the de facto atheist Thomas Hobbes and of the later avowed atheist Jeremy Bentham. Hobbes supposed rights to be mere 'liberties' – opportunities we can seize in the warring state of nature – while Bentham, as Augustine has already discovered, considered them 'nonsense upon stilts' in a world in which man himself is the only conceivable origin of what can questionably still be denoted as the moral law.

Thus, historically speaking, rights are theological, individualist and indicative of some sort of rebellion against previously authoritative institutions. Even granted such historical analysis, however, the truth of which he could hardly deny, our Augustine will soon locate the mines under the surface. In our fallen world, authoritative institutions – not least armies and the police – are unfortunately necessary to preserve even that insubstantial peace which is all that human societies can hope to enjoy, and which is certainly better than nothing; but our Augustine begins to worry that the proliferation of rights-claims, often in competition with each other, even if adequately based in theology, will point towards a disastrous anarchy – and he will note that in that Hobbes agrees with him. He will infer that such anarchy is inevitable if rights are the foundational concept in any project for a re-organization of society.

Perhaps he will look for a compromise that can ensure a principled limitation on rights-claims. He will certainly balk at claims such as that every student has the right to get drunk (as a University of Toronto student newspaper once argued editorially). He may comment wryly – remembering his own resignation from his Chair of Lying (aka Rhetoric) in Milan (C, 9.2.2) – on the appropriateness of a University degree in Sophistry! More seriously, how can any limitation on rights-claims be defended?

Here our Augustine will confront the commonly proposed solution that rights should be extended only to activities that do no harm to someone else. Why, he will ask, if rights are granted by God and by Him built into human nature, should anyone limit the prohibition on harming to harming other people; each agent being himself created in the divine-image should therefore not be deliberately harmed by himself unless such harm – as also harm of another – can be justified on principles acceptable in a theocentric universe. Augustine will wonder whether only atheists could reasonably make the assertion that rights are limited by harm to others – an assertion Christians cannot make. But atheists apparently can have no claim to natural rights anyway, as Hobbes and Bentham both understood.

Augustine will also reject out of hand a common rider to contemporary debate: that we cannot estimate eventual but only immediate damage to others and thus can ignore arguments that the wider society is damaged in the longer term by the granting to certain Hobbesian 'liberties' the status of rights. He will view this self-serving neglect of such persisting effects as fuelled by claims about certainties, future or other, that have always been open to challenge, so that making them – for example to protect pornographers – is sophistic. On the other hand, he will admit that many social goods, being immaterial, cannot easily – if at all – be measured empirically; yet the 'right' to such goods should not be curtailed a priori, as is the judgement of many would-be rights-theorists. We should all have the right (let alone the duty) to worship God in whatever non-abusive way we choose or accept, and the right to protect the life of an unborn human being against the widely asserted 'right' to kill him or her.

Our Augustine will add that both atheist and believer must produce principled reasons, based on a convincing account of what human beings should be, if they are to propose rights at all. If they cannot, then a 'right' looks like a reified and dignified desire, and although some desires might point to rights, others certainly will not. Therefore, we need a standard to separate the two groups, without which there will be as much a right to get drunk or to own a cell phone as to have somewhere to sleep at night.

Our Augustine's concerns, however, will also be metaphysically deep-rooted, for he will want to know what exactly a right is (and what it is not). He has learned, as we have seen, that originally theorists thought of rights as distributed by God; now he frequently hears atheists also asserting them – even sometimes using theological language to do so: thus in the United Kingdom he may hear of our most sacred right to have a National Health Service, and free at the point of delivery. He will detect a muddle in all this and will want to look at the foundation for any and all such claims. A right, he will think, may be claimed deservedly or undeservedly by individuals or groups of individuals; it is something assumed to be recognizable by the mind, yet its presence or absence cannot be empirically verified, except in a trivial sense: if I claim not to be harmed – and others know of my claim – and if I am not harmed, my 'right' will have been respected.

Such and other difficulties will lead our Augustine to infer that rights (if 'natural') must be not just reified desires but some kind of metaphysical entities embodied in individuals, like justice, or goodness. He will also recognize that the analogy with justice does not help with rights, since anyone wishing to deny them can equally well deny the existence of justice; such a one will perhaps think that justice is the advantage of the stronger, or that to say that justice exists is merely to say that just men exist – though that option will not get him very far, unless he can show by what canon we may properly call a man just or unjust.

In fifth-century Hippo, Augustine would have had little difficulty in exemplifying justice: a man is just when he behaves in a loving and godlike way, for all the virtues are modes of love (*The Life-Style of the Catholic Church* 1.15.25) – and similarly with the other virtues, the foundation being God as supremely just or good. With

God left out, our Augustine will feel compelled to conclude that – after all – in a value-free universe rights are what people, or some people, can claim to be able to appeal to, because society allows or encourages them to do so: thus, in the past women did not have the right to vote, but now have been granted that right. In a value-free or atheist world, rights are what those with some sort of authority will find, for whatever reason, socially convenient; some desires will be given the status of a right, others, more or less arbitrarily, not.

Of course, Augustine will recognize that those who claim rights do not think in that way; rather they assume they really *do* have rights – which would be plausible if at least some rights could be shown to be 'natural'. Nevertheless, he will reiterate that without God rights are the liberties that we (or some of us) are willing to accept and grant, for ourselves and for others, and so 'legalize' in our society; perhaps even to grant to (or enforce for) all members of the human race. Thus in a way – God omitted – our Augustine agrees with Hobbes.

Augustine will now sum up: that much contemporary thinking about rights is incoherent; and in at least three respects: where people, contrary to their own supposed principles, treat rights as *more* than merely legal; where rights are constructed by men or groups of men but disallowed by other groups; where de facto atheists encourage belief in rights by the appropriation of religious language and concepts: thus the right to X may be dubbed 'sacred'.

Moreover, Augustine will notice that those who claim their assumed rights will maintain that they *deserve* to be granted the rights they demand; that it would be unjust if these rights were not granted them. Yet it is not at all clear why or when that should be the case. The idea that it is *unjust* for women to be deprived of the right to vote only makes sense in a society – or potential society – in which it is regarded as axiomatic that all adult human beings have an equal right to a say in who governs. Many societies still have not so decided, but it looks as if, whenever 'rights' do get legal recognition, some will infer that legal instantiation reflects a wider supra-human sanction. Clearly, that must be an error in a value-free world; hence, it would appear, as Augustine has already pointed out, that rights are what some people have sufficient power (of force or of persuasion) to secure for themselves and others judged like themselves in some relevant respect.

Augustine will now understand why 'rights' of the unborn, or of the senile, or of those seriously injured and reduced to a 'vegetative state' can be easily denied: these have no power, by force or persuasion (the latter may be called 'oratory') to claim them for themselves. He will disapprove of that situation in that an emotive but unjustified assumption – that of the 'existence of natural rights' – is being used as justification not only for legal rights but also for demanding that the State, subservient to lobbies of the 'strong', *ought* to ensure that only selected people enjoy them.

Augustine has also noticed that rights are claims *against* someone; the implication being that either through ignorance or through malice particular rights, whether claims to or freedoms from are being denied. That must imply that in an ideal society rights-talk would be otiose since all its members necessarily respect their fellows; also that there can be no rights against God, since he must be supposed always to act justly. At this point discussion of rights evolves into discussion of right-religion, but that must be deferred until the next chapter.

There being no rights against God, it follows that although rights were claimed against some authority – whether Church or State – they yet could include no right to autonomy as that would be incoherent: firstly on grounds that we are not capable of autonomy – only God is so capable; secondly, because we *ought not to want* a complete liberty which would imply rights *against God*. This Augustine learns was adduced in the eighteenth century, while in fifth-century Africa he had already suspected it to be the underlying claim of his Pelagian opponents. Yet even in a non-theistic world, since we are unavoidably dependent, the claim to autonomy will be self-destructive and self-deluding. (A nihilist can claim that there is no reason *not* to be self-destructive; we have every 'right' – for want of a better word in this context – so to choose.)

In Augustine's own day and in the Christian centuries which followed – as evidenced for example in the writings of Thomas Aquinas – we have noticed that there was very little discussion of subjective-rights – even though Augustine will find in the 'literature' modern scholars anachronistically attributing rights to Aquinas (and even to himself), thus confusing potentiality with actuality: in that 'X *could* become Y' does not entail that it *will* become Y.

Nevertheless, we must now ask Augustine whether he would prefer to reject rights altogether. His answer will be No. Indeed, in the fifth century he had already acted *as though* there are rights – though he would not have expressed it in that way: in particular the right to worship the Christian God. Yet that 'right' was proposed in the context of what he accepted as fact: namely God's existence, and that in its turn implies that other 'rights' might depend on other related facts: so Augustine will have to consider these other facts, asking himself whether he can propose a revised theory of rights. That theory would need to avoid one of the major problems of contemporary accounts that he has recognized: how to establish a principle by which we allow a right to freedom of religion, but deny a right to get drunk even if we want to.

Whereas much contemporary ethics is founded on rights-theory, in ancient and medieval times it largely depended on the concept of virtue, a tradition that goes back to Socrates who wanted to persuade people that they should seek to make their souls as good as possible. Fourth- and fifth-century Augustine was entirely in sympathy with that: like any Christian, he wanted to end up in God's 'heaven' and for others to fare likewise, and he assumed that the only way to satisfy that desire is to follow God's precepts revealed in the Scriptures as handed down in the Church. He also knew that he could find parallel 'theological' precepts among the better pagan thinkers, because, as St Paul taught, God has written the natural law on our hearts, from which, as he observed, it follows that we all want to be good, to know and love the good; our problem is that we often hardly know what the good is and are too emotionally defective to love it with all the sacrifices such love entails.

Augustine well knows that there are many differences – as typically about humility – between himself and most of his pagan counterparts. He believes that we cannot be virtuous without God's aid and that perfection is impossible in the present life, while the pagans allow that perfection though difficult is not impossible. However, he recognizes there are also great similarities. Both he and the pagans recognize the virtues of courage, self-control, justice and prudence, and however much they disagree (and the pagans disagree with each other) about what is to count as behaviour in accordance with each virtue, they nevertheless all agree that our first duty is to make ourselves virtuous. We have noted Socrates's position, and that if we are Christian (or Jewish), we are commanded by God to love our neighbours as *ourselves*; Augustine will continue to emphasize that we cannot make ourselves virtuous *without* making others also virtuous.

Thus, if we possess the virtue of justice, we will treat other people justly; hence both we and they will know something of what justice is, and from that it is a short conceptual step to seeing that we should be *treated* justly, that we have some sort of 'right' to be treated justly. Similarly with the other cardinal virtues. In short, it is easy to develop a theory about *virtue* into a theory about 'rights': a right to justice is what someone will allow us if he wishes himself and us to behave justly; analogously freedom is the liberty to do what we *ought* to do. Augustine, of course – compared with the pagans – will have even stronger suasion to think in this way, for it is just to treat other people with reference to what they really are, namely created in the image and likeness of God. He will conclude, 'I could have developed – at least I can now develop – my ideas about virtues into theories about rights; what I do not understand is how someone starting with rights-talk can develop a theory of virtue.' How will he defend such a challenging denial?

His first point will be that even without any immediate introduction of God we can argue – as secular philosophers and psychologists could argue – that if we fail to treat others well we shall be damaging our own prospects of a virtuous life. As a Christian, however, he has a further point, one picked up by the early rights-theorists like Grotius and Locke. We shall damage our chances of virtue particularly severely if in our behaviour we fail to acknowledge the importance of the fact that all men are created in God's image; treating them unjustly would not only be offensive to them – depriving them of their 'rights' – but committing blasphemy in not recognizing the image of God. Augustine will add that it is not difficult to understand why modern secularists are still prone to call human rights 'sacred', for 'sacred' they indeed are, although the secularist cannot explain why that is so, and as so often, is caught using a theological idea in a non-theological context, and for its emotional appeal merely, while deluding himself (or being deluded) into thinking he is appealing to some 'natural' good that has no logical justification for appearing on his mental horizon.

We can develop rights-theories from theories of virtue, but the converse does not apply, and the reason is simple and historically intelligible. Rights-theories arose when individuals asserted themselves against some group or organization of their day; historically the claim to rights had little or nothing to do with whether man is a social animal; indeed (like many other contemporary theories, especially neo-Hobbesian contractarianism) it tends to encourage us to deny or at least to ignore that we are social in favour of individualism. More fundamentally, rights-theories at their best are claims about justice, while virtue ethics depends on claims about human goodness, of which justice is only one part. Important though justice has always been among the virtues, any claim to take it seriously depends on what room we have for a transcending goodness. Justice (as Plato already saw) can be derived from goodness; goodness cannot be derived from justice but can only be its root.

Nor is it merely a matter of derivability and of goodness; rights-theories, insofar as they are theories about justice, can have nothing to say about love. Unless we deny that love is (or can be) a good – indeed the supreme good – then virtue theories, insofar as they are theories about goodness, must give an account of love. Augustine will repeat that love is the primary attribute of the Christian God, and that the Platonists had already recognized it as the necessary motor of the best sort of human action. Justice-based theories, in comparison with virtue-theories, must be defective, even, in and of themselves, unworthy of human respect and unquestionably an inadequate foundation for ethics.

Certainly our Augustine thinks of justice as *a* virtue, and he can and will have a place for rights if properly understood – which is to say by reference to justice, which like love is in Augustine's world a divine attribute. People have rights and should be treated justly because they are created in the image and likeness of God – in accordance with the Christian belief that love is God's primary attribute and that human beings are the products of his love. An Augustinian account of rights, as distinct from a secular or pagan derivation, is defensible in terms not of claims about individualism, but in terms only of the love of God. To accept that we have rights is not merely to accept that God is just and that he wishes us to be just, but more fundamentally that God is love and that his love is the only reasonable explanation of why people should have anything like natural rights at all.

In the upshot, Augustine will dismiss much secular talk about rights as the misuse of a theological capital to which the secularist is not entitled. And that is far from all he will maintain. One of the problems with secularized rights-theories is, as we have seen, that there seems little principled way to rule out an endless series of rights-claims: from the right to survive or to be 'free' to the right to get drunk. In Augustine's world that last claim (along with many others) is ruled out: we have no right to get drunk because God does not (at least normally) wish us to be drunk, and he does not wish us to be drunk because he loves us and has created us in his image. Claims to rights are always to be tested as to whether they prepare us for or inhibit us from virtue in the richest Christian sense of that word. We have rights insofar, and only insofar, as the possession of each particular right would make our souls better, or at least prevent them from being harmed by restrictions on our ability to act well. That also explains why (despite the normal view of antiquity and too little appreciation of it in modern times) criminals retain rights too: the right to moral treatment and to behaviour aiming to make them morally better.

8

The Inevitable Irrelevance of Most Contemporary Theology

Theology is necessarily expressed in terms relevant to particular cultures, and some ages and societies are more attuned to it than others. In antiquity, Christians had to establish a new language and a set of new concepts, or at least radically reform older ones, if they were to talk in ways that would come to be denoted 'theology'. By Augustine's time much of that preliminary work had been completed, and indeed it was becoming difficult *not* to think in Christian 'theological' categories, whether in Greek, Latin, Syriac or other ancient languages. Christian culture was superseding paganism in Europe and around the Mediterranean.

The Emperor Constantine is often maligned for making Christianity institutional and 'establishment', but as a result of his so doing many – and for whatever reasons – converted to the new religion. By no means all converts were cynical social-climbers jumping on the Imperial bandwagon; nonetheless, it is matter of historical fact that the religion of the ruler, applied with more or less pressure on the ruled, is a potent factor for social and creedal change. Constantine began to catholicize the Roman Empire by decree. His work was largely to be undone in the southern and eastern Mediterranean lands by the armies of Mohammed and the early caliphs, backing their preaching with sword. So too the Reformation would probably never have succeeded in England without Henry VIII and his successors who protected the reformers for purposes often far from religious. Indeed, without the Elector of Saxony Luther himself would have become liable to the same ultimate ecclesiastical penalty as Huss: being burnt at the stake.

But Augustine Redivivus comes back to a Western world where Christianity is fading fast (even becoming a religion of the oppressed rather than of the persecutors). For more than 200 years he finds the 'West' has been living in a culture that could be described as 'Constantinianism in reverse gear'. And to say that is not to imply that such a change is for the better; indeed Augustine, when he sees it, will find that much has been forgotten or deliberately destroyed. The process of devastation is proceeding, even at an accelerating pace, and political power has been an important driver of the change – at least once the process has begun. After all, in the ancient world, Christian practice, Christian preaching and Christian writing had prepared the way for Constantine, indeed given him a tool for achieving that religious uniformity within the Empire which his predecessors as well as himself had so long desired, even as Voltaire, Hume, Nietzsche and a throng of followers have prepared the way for the present political ascendancy: *cuius regio, eius religio* still applies, though the rulers now are known as 'opinion-formers' and 'liberals'.

And our Augustine will be asked, 'Of which political master do you speak? There is no not-to-be denied Henry VIII or Elizabeth I in modern Britain, nor their likes in other Western States? Don't we hold to a freedom of religion which – up to a point – obtains?' Leaving theoretical questions about freedom of religion aside, our Augustine will note that in 'advanced societies' force does not need to be openly applied: indeed, all societies have their controlling establishments, political history being largely the history of élites, and while we in England are no longer subservient to monarchs like Henry or Elizabeth, nor the French to Robespierre – and although disobeying our masters will not result in immediate torture or an agonizing death – hidden constraints can often be as effective as more open pressures.

Our current political élites are the servants of a pervasive intellectual climate against which it has been made 'politically incorrect' – even 'bad form' – to protest. We are no longer governed by autocratic monarchs but by the more subtle pressures exerted by the 'talking heads' of the largely anti-Christian liberal establishment. But establishments, though officially gentle and caring, cannot flourish without the underlying threat of sanctions

which may begin persuasively but grow ever less violence-free –
and, when applied to those whose beliefs clash with the projects
of the fashionably acceptable homosexual lobbies, may eventually
land Christians in prison, if, for example, they run B and B's but
will not accept homosexual cohabiting on their premises, or if, as
bakers, refuse to put vexatious gay slogans on 'wedding' cakes.

The present theological situation, our Augustine observes, is
the reverse of what obtained in his own day when bishops were
learning to tell secular rulers how to behave, and were in a position
to explain why they had the right to do so. Now the situation is
reversed: theologians – indeed even bishops, cardinals, even popes
seeming impelled to follow the 'correct' opinion in all its variations,
the import of many of which they wholly fail to comprehend –
rather than to form it, being lured, it may be, by a specious claim
that what is 'democratically' tolerant and nonjudgemental is ipso
facto Christian (and it is true that modern European democracy
grew out of initially Christian roots).

Our Augustine will want to understand and explain how this
situation has come about, and he will look first at the late Middle Ages
and the Reformation to find answers. For at that period there were
two subversive pressures on the theological tradition: first, the rise of
voluntarism, which Augustine (as a Platonist) would deny could be
attributed to his influence, but which he would recognize could point
to the decline of philosophical theology insofar as God's acts might
seem to be unintelligible to us, if not actually arbitrary; secondly, the
abandonment of the metaphysical traditions of the Church (damned
as generating ethical Aristotelianism) and the search for a purely
biblical (hence verbal, non-sacramental) theology as anchor for the
Christian faith, or at least for its indeterminate 'spirit'.

Clearly, the second phenomenon is not (and was not) incompatible
with voluntarism, but it also made Christianity dependent on
Everyman's biblical interpretations, which Luther himself, to his
chagrin, found to be infinitely variable, and Augustine will worry
how he himself had become the source of much of the new theology
of the period with his easily misunderstood as well as partly
defective – certainly at times insouciantly formulated – theories of
predestination, but looking back from the beginning of the twenty-
first century Augustine will also be aware that the supposedly
hard-core biblical rock had been undermined by Protestant or ex-
Protestant biblical scholars themselves; to realize with increasing

alarm that the destructive critiques of the Protestants have in time been copied – even exaggerated – by the Catholics, biblical study being viewed as little more than a historical science, with rules of its own which no other kind of historian would accept!

All which developments, our Augustine will realize, add up to the fact that being based on neither tradition nor a seriously meditated account of the Scriptures, theology finds itself with no obvious subject matter, and the Church without her reliable foundational documents or the traditions these represent. Hence, in a trend that had already begun as early as the seventeenth century, Christianity has tended to resolve itself into no more than morality and social justice, and at that same time when secular morality was offering the seemingly more alluring choice between hedonism, conventionalism and nihilism.

None of these, however, sounding even adequately Christian, the Catholic Church has thus gradually tended to evolve – other churches have already completed the mutation – into yet another NGO, albeit tarted up with a hypocritical or even nominal adherence to belief in a transcendent God – or alternatively to a minute devotion to liturgical practices, whether old- or newfangled; the latter are readily mocked in Private Eye's (admittedly Anglican) *Rocky-Horror Service Book*, or the *Bad Vestments* blog: for the former, performed with much outward devotion but little contact with the real world and its needs we (or the older among us) recall Tom Lehrer's *Vatican Rag*. At times Augustine thinks it all looks like a choice between works without faith and faith (in something or other) with scant attention to works. In Scriptural studies he might see us as having to choose between effective denial of the divinity of Christ and a fundamentalist literalism, almost nothing of a principled 'third way' having been established.

In such circumstances Christianity might seem fated to disappear, having little except (in some places) a spuriously fashionable and declining social respectability to encourage new recruits, for whom, however, a more exotic way forward might seem to be Buddhism (also attractive, be it noted, to a number of déraciné intellectuals): a substitute 'Catholicism' not only without a pope (as some suppose is contemporary Orthodoxy) but without institutions and – in practice – often without God; thus an inherited spiritual capital is reformulated and gradually exhausted, leaving only the possibility of secular, materialist and anti-spiritual development.

Our Augustine will sadly contemplate all this working itself out in increasingly banal detail.

His inspection will proceed on three tracks: he will recognize first the gradual disappearance of philosophical (that is, substantially metaphysical) theology; second, the replacement of what remains of metaphysics by a historicism deriving from Hegel in which the present sums up and *replaces* the past (including in its most extreme 'Christian' instantiations, and especially in Germany, the New Testament past); third (and as a consequence), the gradual reconstruction along anti-Christian lines of traditional Christian ethics: the core ethics itself, that is, not merely the appearances under which it was somewhat variably presented to an earlier pagan or neo-pagan world.

He will have heard, for example, that a prominent Anglican archbishop of Canterbury has said he wanted to re-write the whole of Christian sexual ethics; that a prominent Roman Catholic Cardinal bases his account of truth not on the ancient notion that it is higher than the human mind but rather that it 'arises' from a 'dialogue' between the pantheistic Spirit of the Whole and man's increasingly secular awareness. More generally, he will notice that unless when talking among themselves, most Christians are ashamed to acknowledge themselves as such in more than nominal or tribal fashion. And by such non-acknowledging he will point not to an abstaining from forcing one's principles down another's throat in season and out, but to a willingness to sit by silently, with a complacent if not complicit smile, when basic Christian moral principles are decried as stale garbage – and that not by satirists but by do-gooder members of a self-limiting cultural élite. He will watch aghast as he sees how to be accepted by secularists, Christians – and Christian social agencies – have to pander without protest to secularist social programmes, thus inuring themselves to unchristian or anti-Christian solutions to social problems in accordance with what in labour-management dispute-resolutions would be called the 'chin-in-armpit' syndrome of ever blander compromise.

Augustine's first observation – about philosophical theology – will be immediately challenged: surely, it will be observed, there are more people doing philosophical theology than ever before, perhaps indeed as many now as in all previous ages put together. And in a sense that is true: it certainly looks as though Augustine's insistence is still taken seriously that he wants to see in the mind what he believes (T, 15.28.51) and that we should never despise the reasoning powers which God has given us while yet recognizing that unless we believe, all sorts of truths must necessarily be hidden from us.

It is a point on which Augustine had remained steadfast for his entire earthly life; as early as his book *On the Master* (11.37), he had cited the Latin version of *Isaiah* 7:9; 'Unless you have believed, you will not understand.' For to embark on that intellectual journey, he claims, is the only alternative – and then and now we must be brave enough to take it – to ignorance, mere assertion, wishful thinking, and even superstition – errors such as he has already argued must be recognized in much of what passes for contemporary philosophy and theology, and most strikingly perhaps about rights. He will again recall his experiences with the philosophers of an earlier age.

Our 'modernist' may object, with apparently good reason, that what is now termed philosophical theology is carried on in the spirit of Augustine's own original enquiries: we still ask ourselves, for example, what Scripture intends when it speaks of God hardening Pharaoh's heart. Yet there are important sociological differences between the fifth and the twenty-first centuries that should not be forgotten. First, in Augustine's own day, almost all theologians were bishops and whole-hearted believers, and as bishops attention was paid to them. Later, in the middle Ages, they were largely 'religious' and non-episcopal clergy, but they still adopted all the basic teachings of the faith which by then formed the bedrock of their society. Later still, as they allowed that bedrock to crumble, as we have noted, they began to think of Christianity merely as an interesting historical phenomenon of no more intrinsic interest than other such phenomena. So that by now even when they debate (among themselves) such questions as why God hardened Pharaoh's heart, their activities are chiefly relevant to a theological guild and its technicalities rather than to society. Consequently they are generally ignored, where not despised.

Few bishops (being now viewed as diocesan administrators) bother to read what even the better theologians and philosophers write (and which they 'did in graduate school'); that may be in part because it is liable to be trivial; even so this helps to push them further away from meaningful (rather than mere verbal) contact with the older traditions of their own faith and to concentrate on administrative niceties and a secularized and increasingly *anti-*

Catholic sense of social justice. In all this Augustine will recall an item of his own historical past when, still a young priest, he was invited to address the North African bishops *On Faith and the Creed*, and realized he needed to provide an astonishingly elementary lecture.

Here is a second phenomenon which Augustine will notice: in light of the loss of both Bible and Tradition which followed the rejection of Christian metaphysics, the search for understanding began to fade among those on the pews: instead of using faith to develop understanding – *fides quaerens intellectum* – we began unthinkingly to sing how 'faith believes nor questions how': the relevant hymn, adopted by Catholics along with much from Protestantism, symbolizing a rejection of the entire Western intellectual tradition, so largely framed by Augustine himself, of the relationship between theology and philosophy – not to speak of the assistance theology might give to the resolution of difficult philosophical puzzles or apparent puzzles. Augustine will know from his own experience that if Christianity throws away or despises its inherited intellectual characteristics – as some religious orders would seem to have done – it is hardly surprising if its philosophic survivals are dismissed as sham.

And it is not only theory that is abandoned: Our Augustine will have read quite recently a Vatican commission informing us of a breakthrough in Catholic-Jewish relations; Jews are no longer to be proselytized. We must charitably assume the members of the commission were unaware that Augustine had preached this very doctrine, and that many early (though not later) medieval popes had followed his lead, often in opposition to their more theologically primitive or misguided local bishops and laity: he will hope the Vatican was misled by ignorance rather than in hope of a startling headline. Augustine will recall Roman times when it was the foes of Christianity – Celsus, Galen and Porphyry – who charged that Christians were taught not to think, but 'just believe'; true Christian leaders decried any virtue in ignorance.

'Mistakes' of this sort, Augustine will realize, indicate a cultural malaise at times pointing beyond philistinism to barbarism: a more general hostility – even if given a neo-Hegelian coating – to the past and to past wisdom in all its forms – even to correctness of speech or any breath of archaism. He will be shocked to find in many English-language Universities how first-year students are held to find even Jane Austen almost beyond their capacity. The doctrine of progressivism teaches that past glories are not regarded as intrinsically valuable, but mere stages in the history of a decreasingly primitive humanity: thus the history of metaphysics (soon perhaps that of literature) will look like the history of science, of interest only as cultural archaeology, while in ecclesiastical circles 'liberals' already seem to suppose that the Church began with the Second Vatican Council, while even many 'conservatives' will date its origins little further back than the Council of Trent in the sixteenth century. Even at the beginning of the nineteenth century, our Augustine will have found Auguste Comte arguing that the age of religion was being replaced by the age of metaphysics, and that the age of metaphysics is to be succeeded by the age of science. Put all this together – add in the digitalization of human discourse – and Augustine will recognize a radical restriction of the spiritual (as distinct from the material) possibilities available to men and women of the contemporary West.

With regard to ethics, what Augustine would find published as 'theological ethics' would do little to alleviate his concern already expressed. Nor would he have difficulty in identifying further problems in this area, and would recognize that misreadings of his own works have to an extent contributed to them. That is because he has learned that with the arrival of Aristotle's *Ethics* in the Middle Ages a tendency arose to divide morality from salvation, whereas in his own time the two were inseparable. Among the Reformers Calvin supposed that to live by Aristotelian rules (without grace) is the best that is available for the reprobate, while the Christian elect live and are saved by faith.

Augustine will recognize the separation of ethics for the damned – that is, the ethics of Aristotle – from the godly life of the saved, as having led directly to the development of a new ethics of strictly secular nature: a development, he now recognizes, that passed largely unnoticed by the Church, which did little more than denounce some of it as atheist (as in effect it often was), but without pointing out its very specific inadequacies and addressing the increasing inability of theological 'ethics' to rectify them in new and rapidly changing social circumstances. Hence he finds contemporary ethics, whether 'theological' or 'secular', mired in endless controversy, with no agreement in sight as to solutions that could be widely acceptable, and that what is called ethical enquiry –

which includes much theological enquiry – has become an area in which slogans (to be defended even if indefensible) have replaced rationality. Meanwhile Christians are still playing catch-up.

Since contemporary ethics has now, in the West, become largely inoculated against God, Augustine will realize that those theological writers on the subject who are not simple Biblicists (and the apparent sense of the Bible is, of course, often disputed) are often unwise enough to start by accepting (rather than inspecting) the anti-theistic premises of their secular opponents, then, as it were, tacking God on at the end, perhaps as another and superior Person – to which strategy the atheist need only reply that the tacking-on is unnecessary and fails to add any value to the secular solution. Before replying in detail, Augustine will observe that his strictures about secular premises relate not least to the language – the basic vocabulary – in which contemporary theologians accept to carry on their debates with secularists: to illustrate the point, he will point to a curious set of neologisms: the phobia-words, such as Islamophobia, homophobia and transphobia, are coinages introduced into Western jargon to erase any possible criticism of particular phenomena, whether the religion of Islam, or homosexuality, or a fashion for attempting sex-change.

As a skilled rhetorician and debater, Augustine will object that, phobia-words indicating a fear, the question remains as to whether that fear is or is not rational. According to the question-begging usage, it is always posited as to be rejected as irrational, indeed wicked. Augustine will object that he has a legitimate fear of Islam because he finds that it has already destroyed Christianity and imposed itself by violence not only in his own North Africa but along the entire southern and eastern shores of the Mediterranean: it is not irrational, he will assert, for him to be concerned seeing similar destruction threatened to the Christian or post-Christian lands on the northern side of 'our sea'. Similarly with 'homophobia' and 'transphobia': Augustine will assert he is justly fearful because the 'gender-based' actions to which these terms refer are wicked parts of a nihilistic project – conscious or not – aimed at the God-given family – and in the latter case a clear example of modern man's futile attempt to be himself the creator.

Reverting to his main theme, Augustine will observe that the notion that theologians can usefully tack God on to the end of a set of purely secularist calculations from which God has been specifically excluded merely makes Him otiose. He will point out (as he and other Patristic writers did in earlier times) that what the secularists and their would-be theistic fellow-travellers are offering is a travesty of his own approach – which differs from that of Aquinas and the medievals who were writing largely for a more or less homogeneous Christian audience. His own tactic in Hippo was to follow the pagan so far as he could, remaining within the limits of reason but rejecting all question-begging, all ideological sloganeering and all tendentious language, obliging the pagan (as now the secularist) to admit that in the end, without God, he runs up against a brick-wall: and this is now the appropriate tactic in a secularized West.

In his own day, Augustine will point out that the Neoplatonists behaved in an analogous way to some contemporary secularists: driven to realize that men (and women) cannot live the perfect moral life in virtue of their own resources, they fall back on some kind of 'sacramentalism', then called 'theurgy' – whereby to bridge the logical gap. But their sacramentalism, unlike that of the Christians, was based not on historical facts from the life of Jesus and his apostles but on myths developed outside the limits of historical enquiry, such as those of Hercules, Mithras and other purported 'saviours' of mankind: the modern parallels would be Western versions of Buddha or the Hindu gods, or perhaps 'tree-hugging' (Wikka), Druidism (at 'Stonedhenge'), or – more all-embracingly – drug- culture (at Glastonbury). Not that Christian history should be 'rationally' 'demythologized'; indeed to do justice to its full appeal to the whole man it may often need to be 're-mythologized'.

What Augustine repeats theological ethicists should insist on when confronting their secular counterparts is that like the Neoplatonists of old, they will reach a point where their argument runs into the sand; that where the Neoplatonists appealed to a non-historical mythology, they appeal to slogans, often of a scientistic sort: in an earlier discussion he had noted perhaps the most egregious of these: that 'rights are trumps'. Then he admitted that there are indeed human rights (as had been properly recognized by Locke) but that their 'existence' and over-riding claim depends on and can only depend on man's being a creature and created in the image not of himself, nor of some super- or trans-human, but of God. For secular moralists and their contemporary theological 'rivals' who allow themselves to fall back on fundamentally secular premises, the basic problem is that they fail to recognize that what they want to demonstrate is indemonstrable with the resources they allow themselves: hence the slogans and ideology which deny any honest recognition of success for the theist and failure for the secularist.

Worse than the failure in the science of theological ethics itself, Augustine continues, is the effect of such failure on our understanding of the human person. Modern ethics, he notes – in this quite different from proper theological ethics – tends to depersonalize human beings, to homogenize them and treat them as units in hope to offer a morality which would treat all of us not only as of equal value but of indistinguishable character: distinctions of history, of culture, even the distinction between males and females, all are to disappear in the pursuit of a pseudo-egalitarian concept of justice. In aiming at such a result the secularist (and the would-be theist insofar as he follows the secularist's lead) is painting a picture of the human being from which all individuality, and a fortiori all spirituality, is ultimately cleansed, being ignored or debunked. Our Augustine has already remarked that justice, though assuredly a virtue, is not, in Christian terms, the highest of the virtues; that place is reserved for love, and it is of the essence of love not to eliminate the particular features of the object of love, but to admire and seek to promote their very uniqueness.

As he noted in the very first of his addresses to our contemporaries, Augustine is always reminding us of what we now call the first-person stance. He believes that to describe the contents of the world, it is insufficient merely to give a third-person scientific description: for example, to say that there are so many millions of human beings inhabiting our planet. It is essential to give such information, of course, and it is available; but it is important to add that the way each of us views the world – his or her world – is part of the totality to be accounted and described, even though none of us can ever begin to do this – let alone account for the billions who have gone before. He reminds us that he was aware of this both when he wrote the *Confessions*, in which he described his own personal view of the world, his own experiences and his own unique relationship to God, and in *The City of God* where he insisted that to understand the universe we need to consider not only metaphysics (as the Neoplatonists in particular had done) but also history as viewed, he would hope, through a theological lens. Thus, in his own writings had he composed first-person accounts of himself and also of his historical culture and society.

For it is important to understand what is lost if such material is omitted from any supposedly full account of the contents of our world – and at this point Augustine's challenge, not least to theologians, is surprising, indeed shocking: he will argue that scientific accounts are homogenized, that with lack of attention to personal and cultural features man's real and spiritual dimension is eliminated – that, with Christian spirituality lost, theology too, far from its erstwhile claim to be the queen of the sciences, is left – designedly – without significant role in human life. Spirituality depends on recognition of human diversity; and diversity begins with its most basic distinction between male and female: a distinction given too little weight and too little reflection by serious thinkers – and here Augustine makes a rare bow to modernity – before our own times. He adds that with the loss of spirituality we lose not only religion but art, music and literature *qua* art – that is, properly so- called – indeed all that depends on a recognition and respect for inspirational beauty (rather than merely for good technique).

In his own writings, Augustine reminds us, he has noted the differing spiritualities of Peter and Mary Magdalene, the latter being 'superior in affect' (S, 229L.1; JG, 121.1), and to indicate the importance of this difference he has pointed to the Christian idea – already traditional in the fifth century, and especially developed by Origen – that in relation to God all human souls must 'somehow' be female: more difficult, he might add ruefully, for males, but to be accepted as necessity, as a corollary of what he has written about Mary Magdalene. It is more difficult for males, he repeats, because on the analogy with sexual relations, an essential feature of such relations is that the male aims to 'conquer', the female to be 'conquered' (better: 'to be receptive') – while in relation to God all, male and female alike, must recognize that we cannot dictate terms to God but must accept God's loving terms for us, which are always in our own best interest.

In the more homogenized modern world, our Augustine will continue, it is not only that sexual love is increasingly reduced to lust, or more trivially to 'fun', but that even friendships are rendered more and more implausible and ephemeral, being often assumed – against the wisdom of earlier times – to be overtly or covertly homoerotic: in any case, who can trust a friend who may be thought of as a 'serial self', and thus unable to make any commitments. Such an unsubstantial or homogenized human is capable of neither love nor friendship, nor even of genuine thought, for which he may be induced to substitute slogans, sometimes the more effective if indefensible. Indeed, he or she comes only by courtesy or genes to be described as human: we claim and aspire to be super-humans, but we finish up as subhumans: not animals, since we were intended to be more than animals and could never be identified with them, but a debased, 'consumerist' race whose spirituality is to be nourished by the most up-to-date Hollywood idol, spouting words of wisdom as he or she leaves a night-club and affirms her (or more usually his) individuality by urinating in the street. Or perhaps not: that would be so 'sixties!'

Augustine will condemn all contemporary theologians who press not simply for an equal evaluation of males and females but for their essential and absolute identity, sexual differentiation being pure accident – the product of social discourse, and therefore subject to choice among human beings: for in that case, even if we are born seemingly male, we have every 'right' – against God (as Augustine would put it) – to choose to be female. The claim that biological sex can be overcome by choice of 'gender' is a way – increasingly favoured by desiderate theologians – for us to be self-creators so far as it is scientifically possible and well beyond that. Put otherwise – though Augustine has not formally so pronounced but in line with his thought and applying it – we are created as rational and emotional animals who live under God's established laws of nature: we can correct and strive to heal obvious malformations and malfunctions but cannot (and should not even dare so to wish) override the basic determinations of our God-given nature. Augustine is disturbed by 'theologians' who, having abandoned tradition and Scripture, have fallen into such postmodern secular self-worship: ultra-Pelagians, further tainted by scientism.

Ah, comes the reply from the theological guild, we have not banned the Bible nor abandoned Christian traditions entirely. To which Augustine replies:

> In my earlier incarnation I wrote a literal commentary on *Genesis*, not because I believed that the world was literally formed in six days but because I wanted to insist that the Scriptures must be

accorded some historical reality or they are worthless: I knew
that theologians (I myself before I learned better) would explain
away passages of Scripture they did not like by appealing to
allegory, but had no principled explanation of when such appeals
to allegory should be made. A similar situation pertains in an
even more extreme version today, when there is virtually nothing
left of the account of man given in the Scriptures immune to
the fantasies and lusts of post-modern man. If theologians (let
alone historians of religion) still pay lip-service to the Scriptures,
it is often on condition they be interpreted recklessly and in
accord with the most recent ethical and psychological fads. It is
hardly surprising that theology has become both despised and
irrelevant – or rather despised because irrelevant.

Thus our Augustine's conclusions will be simple and devastating:
most modern theology has become radically reductionist (where it is
not mere sentimentality), the reduction being guaranteed the applause
of a secular culture basically hostile not merely to Christianity, but to
any form of theism, transcendental metaphysics, or what in the past
was called spirituality. The latter, Augustine will observe again has by
now a marked tendency – driven by individualism – to degenerate into
tree-hugging or a sentimental love of animals (sometimes patently
substituted for human beings). The only 'Christian' alternative on
offer in the twenty-first century seems to be declaratively pious
'fundamentalism', which both denies the intellectual traditions of
Christian theology and philosophy and ignores or even denigrates
God's gift of reason itself.
    Here Augustine will sum up: Theology either is the queen of
the sciences or is nothing, while too many of its contemporary
practitioners – in the absence of traditional foundations in the
practice of the Church and in the Scriptures – find no option but
slavery to every passing intellectual passion, even every fashionable
lust. In short, they forget what he has pointed out many times,
as at length in The City of God, that there are two 'loves', for
God and for one's selfish self, and that those two have founded
two radically incompatible 'cities'. Nevertheless – unfortunately,
indeed disastrously – though the earthly city has been developed in
contempt of God, and regularly shows itself to be so, it is appeased
by many contemporary 'theologians'. Perhaps part of the problem
is institutional: perhaps, for example, there are too many residual

religious orders that finding their original role unnecessary or boring have little to do but reach for a dissident notoriety. Augustine remembers writing in one of his early letters that in his first years of conversion he thought of himself as a first-class, élite Christian, seeking quietly to 'deify himself'; later, while remaining a monk, he regretted his earlier contempt for the less exotic, more run-of-the-mill and 'active' cathedral clergy.

9

Austin's 'Brag': Conventional Relativism, Nihilism or the Catholic Tradition?

My charge is ... in brief, to crie alarme spiritual against foul vice and proud ignorance, where-with many of my dear Countrymen are abused.

EDMUND CAMPION

In 1581, before composing his *Ten Reasons* (*Decem Rationes*) explaining the theological defects of the newly reconstructed Church of England, the Jesuit scholar Edmund Campion published what opponents – not unreasonably – dubbed his *Brag*, in effect inviting the Council of Queen Elizabeth I to restore England to the 'Old Faith' and informing the 'reformed' clergy that he was willing to debate with any and all of them and of the reasons why he would win, 'for the enterprise ... is of God'. In true Elizabethan style the Protestants declined to take up his challenge until he had been so severely tortured that he could hardly stand, though even then they failed to win the debate, which instead produced converts, including the Earl of Arundel, St Philip Howard. In producing a *Brag* of his own in the twenty-first century, Augustine faces no immediate threat of racking, hanging, castration and disembowelling (though given the intolerance and potential totalitarianism of the Western liberal mind, we might be less sure of his fate in years to come); still, his task, in confronting the secularism that marks the last stage of the Protestant disintegration of faith so feared by Campion, would in many respects be remarkably similar to that faced by the sixteenth-century Jesuit martyr.

That may seem puzzling: there are no merciless monarchs with their array of informers and torturers to intimidate the present critic of Western modes of thinking. Yet the challenge our Augustine faces is hardly less daunting. When the Catholic martyrs of the sixteenth century were reported butchered, it was customary among the exiles at the English College in Rome to sing a *Te Deum* – as did Campion when convicted – while others condemned might sing 'This is the day of the Lord, let us rejoice in it.' Both the threat, and the raw courage required to stand firm, are obvious enough, but moral courage may be more readily enfeebled than physical courage, and though our Augustine need fear no summary butchering (albeit if in clericals he might be spat on or assaulted in our streets – as has happened to clerics known to the present writer), he will certainly risk being despised or ignored: excluded from *bien pensant* coteries, condemned as a bigot (or fascist, or 'homophobe'), denied invitations to 'High Table' or to a Hampstead brasserie. Active Christians are at times accorded a minimum of respect – when they say 'the right' things – but are more normally treated with contempt, if in less impolite language than that of Nietzsche: 'You can almost smell those Christian agitators.' In the university world, at least in Britain, Augustine would face less immediate violence (verbal or otherwise) than curt dismissal as an irrelevant voice from a superseded past.

Which of course he appears to be, and his *Brag* will remind his readers of the relevance of what they have forgotten, and the devastating personal and social effects of their forgetfulness. In listing what has been lost or thrown away, Augustine will start with the broadest items – the architecture of the house, as we might put it – then pass to specific pieces of furniture and an unblinking look at what of spiritual value can persist amid the rubble.

First and most obviously he will lament the massive decline – unparalleled in history – of the belief in any kind of transcendent God, to be substituted by what Christians realize can only be the idols of hedonistic, nationalist or utilitarian worship. His detractors will retort that there is no loss here, only the overdue removal of primitive superstition. Ignoring them, Augustine will invite us to look at the unfortunate effects of godlessness, pointing to the mental and moral changes wrought by the mass abandonment of Christianity. Thus his *Brag* will highlight the rejection of history and of objectivity, the loss of religious support for moral assertions, the debasement and disintegration of the concept of a human person.

Augustine will remind us that Christianity is not just a transcendental metaphysic like some forms of Platonism, but also a historical sequence of events which implies the importance of historical time, the times of ancient Israel, then those crucial early years of our era in which Jesus lived and died. The importance of this history, he will continue, is that it focuses not on humanity as such, but on the particularities of a life in a community long established as chosen by God for his redemptive work; that, he will note, indicates the human dimension of Christianity, which has to do with us as individuals rather than (or at least as well as) that abstract 'humanity' much beloved by our secular do-gooders.

Augustine wants to combine history with metaphysics, so will be particularly insistent that the historical content of Christianity through the ages be given the closest attention – repudiating the anti-historical stance of many contemporary theologians. But he will also insist that without metaphysical foundations reflection on God must be fundamentalist at best, otherwise wishful and sentimental dreaming. For though he accepts that metaphysics is not enough, he will reiterate that it is not only desirable but essential; so transcendent but non-Christian divinity is more salutary than deity's absence.

Augustine will have become more acutely aware of the necessary relationship between metaphysics and history when he reflected on the spiritual history – rather: spiritual decline – of a number of prominent French clergy from Loisy to Hadot in the past two centuries: brought up as conservative Catholics, they first dropped the history to move from Christianity to some sort of transcendental Platonic 'spirituality' not only without history but without human institutions. His own historical self, Augustine will remember, was tempted in the same way, especially in his early more Neoplatonic days when he hoped to live as a detached member of the new 'Christian' élite.

Next, our French clerics dropped the transcendence, leaving them with a somewhat more benevolent version of ancient Stoicism: a quasi-vitalist metaphysic to be impossibly squared with the 'demythologized' natural world of post-sixteenth-century scientific man. Yet ancient Stoicism was no *subjectivist* construction, and Augustine will remark that our present subjectivism looks like a caricature of his own emphasis on the fact that our *beliefs* about what there is are part of what there is. Such a caricature must lead, and has led, to the wholesale denial of objective truth; yet we are what we are, not only what we might suppose ourselves to be.

With the loss of transcendence Augustine finds an increasing denial of 'lesser' forms of objectivism: in philosophy we have often denied the objective reality of the world in which we live, claiming that all we know is sense-data, not the 'things in themselves' which lie behind. So he will identify once again two features of our present collective mentality, both of which he has touched on in previous sections of these his reincarnated labours: first, that we still long for our lost objectivity, at least in the moral area; we want to be able to say that 'genocide' really is *wrong*, not simply unpleasant or uncomfortable or undesirable; second that we are disconcertingly prone to assume that because we cannot know the 'essence' of something – say a piece of iron – we know nothing about it at all. This latter attitude, common among our post-modern gurus, is an obvious mistake: it is true that to know what iron is will often in practice boil down to knowing what one can do with a piece of iron (such as make a tool). Yet that is still knowledge, however limited. And our mere ability to know that we can make a blade of iron and not out of clay or flour indicates not only that we do indeed have some kind of knowledge, but also that it is not true that 'knowing' what iron is merely amounts to knowing how to deploy a mode of discourse engendered by a particular culture: which of course it is, but not all that it is.

Our Augustine will now pass to further effects of our slide from transcendental religion to what increasingly tends towards solipsism. One of the more significant of these will be the loss of any objective content for the moral sense; hence an inability to form the 'conscience' objectively: appeals to conscience will be reduced to appeals to 'sincerity'. Augustine will not deny that we – or most of us – still possess a moral sense, that is, an awareness that there is a significant difference – somehow intelligible – between right and wrong: thus he will note again that as yet few of us would say that the Holocaust was inconvenient (though it certainly was for many), or that it did not contribute to the greatest good of the greatest number (it was in fact designed to do precisely that), or that we just do not like hearing about it; he will insist that we will want to say that it was incontrovertibly *wrong*. But when he then asks what it means to be 'wrong', he finds no adequate answer available which, in his view, does not ultimately point to the God whose existence is widely denied – not necessarily to the Judeo-Christian God in the first instance, but certainly to some transcendent source of value. He then observes that in a more rational age it was precisely because theologians thought (however inadequately) about that source of value that they were reasonably able to claim that their profession should be recognized as Queen of the Sciences.

All of which will be disputed, and Augustine will be told that there is no necessary connection between any religion (let alone the worship of a transcendent God) and morality. He will ignore that, merely commenting, it may be, in the words of Nietzsche, that we have not got rid of God because we have not got rid of grammar – or with the claim of Dostoievski that without God there are no limits on what we can 'morally' attempt. His stance, like Nietzsche's, that it is impossible even to *argue* without admitting the importance of grammatical intelligibility, is an anti-relativist argument which goes back to Plato, hence to the very origins of what was to become Christianized philosophy. Nietzsche cannot avoid grammar in arguing for a godless – that is, unintelligible – world, but once intelligibility is admitted – particularly in the world of moral or aesthetic evaluation – he knows his structure will collapse unless allowed ultimately to depend on something external to the Universe, that is, transcendent: on what we call God.

*

When Feuerbach in the nineteenth century argued to his own satisfaction that he had shown that 'God' is always a projection of human wishes, some of his critics challenged him that it is not enough to get rid of a transcendent God; the same sort of arguments must be deployed against the notion of the unique individual person, or 'self'. Feuerbach took this criticism seriously, as (albeit for different reasons) will our Augustine: because, that is, he wants to emphasize the unique role and importance of the individual human being, not just of humanity as such. He will admit that the notion of the 'person' (not least of the person as a combination of soul and body) remains mysterious: he thinks that we both know ourselves and know that we cannot know ourselves – let alone understand ourselves – outside a religious framework, thus developing an idea, as he has already told us, that he found in some of the Neoplatonists, especially in Plotinus's saying that we do not know who we are because we do not know – or rather have forgotten – our 'father': that is, the source of our individual being. As a result of that ignorance, and tending to deepen it, we try crazily to project ourselves as self-creators.

And our Augustine will also 'brag' of his dissatisfaction with many of the more traditional axioms still offered in response to modern accounts of the dissolution of the 'self'. Thus looking back from his twenty-first-century standpoint he will read that according to Boethius we are 'individual substances of a rational nature', and he will find Boethius's account still widely accepted by Christian thinkers – or it may be misinterpreted. He himself (perhaps agreeing with Boethius against some of latter's admirers) wants to understand 'rational' not in terms of an aridly Cartesian account of the mind, but from the Platonic standpoint he has always professed, whereby to be 'rational' entails not only to possess cognitive but also emotional powers. Thus to be rational about God will imply not only to know that God exists, but also to know him as ultimate object of human love.

Finding that 'correction' about knowledge – Platonic in its origin – widely ignored, Augustine will observe that to know ourselves is to recognize ourselves as cognitive, loving and *dependent* animals. And that 'dependence' will have to be cashed out to imply that we depend on not only on God, but on other humans – all being 'in the image and likeness of God' – if we are to develop our fully and uniquely human capacities. Only in such interrelationship can we move from mere atomic identity to genuine personhood.

We need to integrate our semi-autonomy – for we have some sort of capacity to accept or reject God and the Good – with a dependence on others that can only be realized by some sort of willed self-gift. For we are neither autonomous individuals nor simply a collection of relations, but persons who grow from our conception through first instinctive, then ultimately intentional existence for others as well as for ourselves. Again Augustine will recall how in his early days in North Africa, under the influence of the Plotinian dictum that we should strive to be alone with the Alone, he found it easier to profess 'the first and greatest commandment' – that we should love the Lord our God – than the second – that we should love our neighbour as ourselves (albeit 'in the Lord'), but that he eventually recognized that since the world is God's product and we all are in God's image, the second commandment is the logical extension of the first.

But with God removed and the self dissolved, as Feuerbach was persuaded to believe necessary, some wholly other version of human nature – or non-nature – will be found to prevail in the contemporary world – absurdly: Augustine will look at the options and will not be impressed as once again he recalls three wholly inadequate accounts circulating among professed thinkers:

1   That we are just material bodies and all our mental, aesthetic and 'spiritual' activities simply activities of the brain. That he will dismiss as failing to account even for some of the most obvious human phenomena: thus he himself can be described in material terms as fat or thin, but scarcely as just or unjust. That being so, he will observe that we have either to fall back on the notion that all such qualities as justice are simply the way in which we, subjectively or in groups, represent *material* experiences – which thus have no enduring interest or importance – or that the world is to be explained (something after all in the manner of the ancient Stoics) as vitalist; he will find such ideas now sometimes dubbed 'dual aspect theory', and that they are merely claims that matter has in fact other properties which in our present state of scientific knowledge we cannot discover, let alone explain. He will realize that there is little need to reject this kind of vagueness since in its 'scientific' version it will never long hold the attention of more than a few theophobic professors desperate to preserve at least some version of materialism.

2   Augustine will also hear people claiming that we are 'Cartesian' egos, so reducing each of us to an immaterial self that might seem to be angel rather than human being. Hence he will find no reason to suppose he was wrong to denote us some kind of 'radical' mixture of soul and body which he called a 'person' (L, 137.3.11): a term already susceptible of Christian implications and now designating

a spiritual and bodily whole with only conceptually distinguishable powers or features, such as memory, understanding and love. For just as our immaterial aspect cannot be airbrushed out to satisfy a materialist model, so on a Cartesian model it is our material aspects which pose the serious problem. And there is more: by now, as we have noticed, Augustine will have read enough Hume to have found sympathetic the Scottish sceptic's complaint that by Cartesian introspection he can never find the static inner self, that 'ego', which consciousness is supposed to indicate, but instead always finds himself doing something, thinking or feeling. Nevertheless, he will also recognize that Hume drew the wrong conclusions from his compelling criticism of Descartes, adding that Thomas Aquinas, like himself, would realize that the Cartesian self is not only too aridly rational but also too static, too inert.

3   Hume's alternative notion, appropriated by various contemporary thinkers, that we are serial selves will fare little better, implausibly abandoning as it must any notion of commitment to one's own past: an effect, Augustine will note, particularly attractive in the contemporary world even where its philosophical origins are unknown: for many will think it profitable to hold that there is no reason or continuing obligation to keep a promise, or respect any kind of previous commitment, if one is no longer the same person as the he or she who made it.

Perhaps Augustine will conclude that Aristotle has done better – and recognize that he had been unwise to follow Plotinus in holding that Aristotle's attempts to resolve the soul–body problem could be so easily disposed of. For Aristotle was right to assume that it is the very combination of an immaterial soul and a material body which needs to be explained. Yet Augustine will still worry that Aristotle seems to think he has achieved more than he has, for how, he might ask, is it possible for an immaterial soul to give commands to a material body? Somehow, man is still being misdescribed and a dualistic vision has still not been entirely exorcized.

What Aristotle seems to miss, Augustine will find, is that the immaterial soul, being a part of the 'whole' person, *loves* and must *love* the material body; there must be a 'sweet marriage-bond of body and soul' (L, 140): 'My flesh shall be my friend throughout eternity' (S, 155.14.15). Or again (S, 344.4): 'I know you want to go on living. You do not want to die. You would like to pass over from this life to another in such a way that you would not rise again as a dead man, but alive and changed for the better. Somehow the soul itself wishes and desires it'... So Augustine cites *Ephesians* 5.29, 'No one hates his own flesh'; and again: 'the whole preaching and dispensation given through Christ is this and nothing else: the resurrection – resurrection not only of soul but of body' (JG, 23.6).

That sort of approach may induce our Augustine to find Plotinus and the Neoplatonists not *entirely* wrong in their anti-Aristotelianism, since they taught that the body is 'in' the soul and hence ultimately – and for a Christian lovingly – controlled and commanded by the soul. Thus in the end he will wonder whether he has perhaps begun to light on a theory to explain not only the unity of the person but its qualitative uniqueness – an absolute prerequisite, as he has shown us, from a Christian point of view for which the love of the soul for the body shadows in some sort the intra-Trinitarian love of the divine persons, in whose image we are.

Of course, the theory of the person which Augustine now seems to need must not only be convenient and coherent; it must also be true. He will at least be clear that the modern alternatives are all radically reductionist – and the systems of morality built around them also radically reductionist, and therefore necessarily false; hence to teach them is to teach what is false, thus paradoxically unchristian: he has long since identified Truth with Christ, who alone can reveal the intelligibility of the world we inhabit and ourselves as its inhabitants.

The parallel to reductionism in the psychological and metaphysical sphere is propaganda in the political sphere. It is of the essence of 'good' (that is, effective) propaganda that what it claims is not totally false; we can be sucked in by a small amount of truth, even when that small amount is exaggerated so as to swamp all other important (and by the propagandist discounted) features of the situation evoked. And just as the political propagandist will come to believe his own propaganda, so the reductionist metaphysician or anti-metaphysician will come to believe that the little he believes is all that there is.

Our Augustine will conclude his *Brag* by summing up the options for those who reject the claims he makes once again for

Christian faith, and these options are but two: a conventionalism spiced with relativism, or nihilism. The first of these he will dismiss as sub-human, for it urges us to accept uncritically the belief systems that come and go around us: this, he will remind us, is to reject Socrates's wholly proper claim that the unexamined life is sub-human (*Apology* 38a); living in that way we have from the value point of view little to distinguish us from ants or other social insects. And since any convention is acceptable, he concludes that *qua* convention all are equally worthless, adding that to believe that a life of this sort is autonomous is laughable; the best that could be said of it is that so living we may be *deluded* into thinking ourselves autonomous, while being little better than more or less ineffective puppets on the stage of an ever-changing play composed by ever-changing authors.

Autonomy, of course, fares better – or seems to – with the nihilist option; since nothing matters except ourselves – and that in itself seems absurd – we can try to make ourselves as autonomous as the nihilist dreams to be: a self-creator, though all the nihilist can create is his own moral mutilation and eventual death, 'preferably' by suicide, seen as being the only possible 'free' act. Augustine will comment sadly that he is not surprised by the increase in the number of suicides – especially among the young, whose energies are thus dissipated into a 'culture of death' – and among ageing professors – and he is even more saddened that the young have been regularly misled by the self-indulgent, even self-worshipping, professors.

An underlying theme to which Augustine will return in his *Brag* is that we have forgotten so many truths with which we were once familiar – as Campion must have realized that his task of recovering England for the 'old faith' was made immeasurably more difficult by the fact that generations were being born who had never known, and were being taught not to want to know about that earlier and saner world. Like Campion, Augustine has a huge task confronting him; unlike Campion he will recognize that he had always predicted such difficulties in 'this darkness of social life' if the fourth-century Christianization of the West were ever to be reversed. And he will remember that having to struggle against forces we do not know can be overcome in our lifetime was always part of his account of our human predicament – yet the struggle is tempered by hope for an eventual future.

At the end of Austin's *Brag* its author will recall how at the end of his life, he tried to revise his work so that it could provide no comfort for his spiritual enemies. The immediate future looked dark, though he probably underestimated how much even his corrected writings would be perverted by his Christian successors. In 2018, he will be aware that the risks for the human race of reverting to a subhuman condition (thus deliberately undoing the latter stages of the evolutionary process), or of killing itself off by trying to be superhuman, are even greater than he supposed them in that earlier part of the fifth century which inaugurated the collapse of most of what he perceived as the stable pillars of a society which was, and would long remain, and even flourish, as substantially Christian.

Transcript of a Radio Interview with Bishop Austin Redivivus: 1 April 2016

ANNOUNCER: As listeners may know, from among the thousands of African migrants rescued from the seas around Sicily has emerged a man who, speaking in Latin and wrapping the proffered blanket round him toga-wise, appeared to be claiming refuge from the dissolution of the old Roman Empire. An interpreter being found and his mistake being explained, the seeming time-warp appeared less to him surprising than to his rescuers, since, as he gave them to understand, he had acquired from those he referred to as the Supernal Powers (possibly therefore connected to the Chinese) some advanced mode of time travel and the remit to report on the state of the Western world as he should find it. Though he was duly debriefed by EU Security officials, little more could be learned and it was thought best to supply him with minders who would observe and report on how he would perform his putative mission, due notice having been given to the FBI, NATO, our own MI6 and – er, Mossad.

Since being pulled from the sea on 28th August last, Bishop Austin Redivivus, as he has given out his name, has shown himself quick to learn the English language – if with some archaism acquired from the Elizabethan period in which he has taken a great interest – as well as Italian and Greek, in both of which he had already some background, enabling him to converse with both the Pope and the Ecumenical Patriarch. However, that tongue in which he is most fluent being Latin, we have engaged the help of that well-known Classicist Professor Pitt Bones for the purposes of this recorded and edited interview. We shall also have input from the well-known Historian Professor Dove Key-Starr who has kindly agreed to be with us on a link from the well-respected Chattering School of Social Studies. And of course we have our familiar anchor-man, Jim Summe-Geeze. Over to you, Jim.

JIM: Bishop Redivivus – or perhaps I may be permitted to refer to you familiarly as Austin?

AUSTIN: Indeed, Sir, that is our Roman custom.

JIM: Thank you – Austin. Now we understand you have spent some months among us, initially in Italy and Greece, then Germany and the whole of this Hilary term as guest of All Souls College, Oxford. Perhaps you will tell our listeners what has most surprised you about the modern Europe you have come to know, with its many inventions undreamed of in your day: this radio that enables us to bring you live to so wide an audience … the car, the aeroplane, to name a further two of the most prominent of our technological triumphs!

AUSTIN: Indeed so, and I admire *almost* unreservedly all these conveniences…

KEY-STARR: Yes, that must be an obvious one! [*Austin looks puzzled; Jim gives a forced laugh.*]

JIM: Yes, Dove; I'm sure our listeners appreciate your humour! Never mind, Austin, just keep telling us.

AUSTIN: It is a long task! But leaving aside what you refer to as the technological triumphs of modernity: initially most striking was to find a Europe centred more on the north, on the barbarian lands of the Teutones and the Britannici, as well as their extensions beyond the shores of the Great Ocean and to lands in my time merely fabled. It was some satisfaction to find that the menacing hordes of invaders had been largely converted to the True Faith. It was for that I prayed as I lay dying…

JIM [*embarrassed*]:   Ah yes, well… Charlemagne and all that… That was a long time ago! You must find things very different now, Austin?

AUSTIN: Different indeed! Sadly so – though I will not say in *all* respects worse…

JIM: Surely in very many ways better! At the risk of embarrassing you and for listeners who may have heard no more about you, I must point out that you rather notoriously encouraged persecutions. We do not now persecute, you know!

AUSTIN: And yet you have had within this Europe and within still-living memory persecution more vile and unjust than any I could have envisaged! In Germany and beyond I visited the sites of the so-called Holocaust of Christ's own people, the Jews...

JIM: Ah yes! But that cannot happen again!

AUSTIN: Had I been heeded it could not have happened at all – not in my name who taught that the Lord's own nation were not even to be proselytized: that having antecedently God's Truth they were to await His Coming.

JIM: Really?

AUSTIN: By Providence you have still my writings to prove it. As also setting forth my views on the needful restraint of those pervicacious in setting themselves up in opposition to God's Revelation and Truth.

JIM: Ah – yes, well... You'll have realized that most of us no longer believe in all that – with the Advance of Science on so many fronts...

AUSTIN: So they all tell me at All Souls – in despite of that institute's name! – but not what this all-wise Science can tell us – more, that is, than about the workings of existent things. In which truly they display the wonders of Creation more than in my day could begin to be unfolded, howsoever it might be guessed at! Yet mistaking, perchance, Creation for its Creator?

JIM: But we see no evidence for a Creator.

AUSTIN: And yet is it all around you, as it ever was, and the more marvellously displayed by your Science! Which it seems has turned less to wonder than to manipulation, receding from its origins in the Latin *scientia*, meaning Knowledge.

JIM: Yes, well – sadly our time is limited and ... Descartes – though a Catholic of sorts – and among ourselves Sir Francis Bacon is the man for you there, if ever you should encounter him in your time-travels.

AUSTIN: So they have told me at All Souls, and pointed me to his works. I confess he is thus far unknown in the country wherefrom I come ... as might be on account of his having been to the forefront of the persecutions in this nation and his time?

DOVE: The glory times of Queen Bess, of whom Bacon was a minister, and with Cecil guided the ship of state safely through the Reformation!

AUSTIN: Not without persecutory violence, as I understand on both sides. And since you have challenged me on the subject, I notice a subtler form of persecution than rack and rope beginning to prevail against Christians of various stripes. I read how such basic Christian – nay, such basic human values as those of life itself and natural marriage are being denied and even sanctioned in favour of...

JIM: Sadly, Austin, those are topics beyond the remit of this programme, being highly disputatious and the BBC Charter enjoining on us to foster consent...

AUSTIN: Consent of the whole British people? Or all speakers of English? Or of the whole world? That were indeed best obtained by the persecutions, whether or not subtle, of which we have been speaking!

JIM: Consent, of course, of those best qualified to know what is best for us! The educated classes: writers, journalists, professors, even bishops. I realize that you yourself own to the title of Bishop, but...

AUSTIN: Indeed, in my day also there were such presumptuous men puffed up with pride – professors and even bishops, as Julian of Eclanum and the monk Pelagius: with both of these I held controversy as I saw them lead souls to perdition. I perceive their doctrines of the inherent capacity of man for salvation have gained great ground in this land of the Britannici.

JIM: Yes, well, we have been a very self-reliant nation: that is what has kept us largely out of trouble. You see, Austin, in the long centuries between your day and this just about everything has been tried: Church, Empire, in the East Caesaropapism, in the West the Reformation, followed by compromise: *cuius regio, eius religio*... Professor Bones will perhaps translate.

PITT BONES: Certainly – ah, *cuius*: gender *communis* in genitive case of relative pronoun *qui, quae, quod*: of whose. Similarly *eius*: common gender in genitive of personal pronoun *is, ea, id*: he, she, it. Thus *cuius... eius*: aforesaid pronouns used co-relatively to yield: *of whose... of his/hers/ its*. I trust that is clear enough thus far for your listeners?

JIM: Could not be clearer, I'm sure! Perhaps you would care to translate?

PITT: To be sure – we are coming to that! Then '*regio*', hence our 'region', and '*religio*' – literally that which binds – hence our 'religion'. Yielding *cuius regio, eius religio* – the admirably concise encapsulation of the *de facto* upshot of the Wars of Religion: whoever rules decides on his (or her) region's religious affiliation!

AUSTIN: I could not have put it better, professor Bones! You show a wonderfully precise understanding of our Latin tongue! *Cuius regio, eius religio* – familiar to my day as Caesaropapism. I myself could never countenance that the religious preferences of a ruler should bind his or her subjects regardless of Truth...

JIM: Truth – but what is that? As that same Francis Bacon asks at the outset of one of his Essays.

AUSTIN: I have read it. He quotes Pontius Pilatus.

JIM: Just so! Every man has his own Truth – and of course every woman... Hence in our time we have agreed – or the great majority of us – to leave everyone to his or her preference, his or her rights as we now see it. Within reason, that is.

AUSTIN: Reason! You should ask, as of Truth, What is that? These words would appear to have been robbed of their reference and so of much meaning! Reason in man is the glimmering light of his brotherhood with the Logos of God; Truth is One or it is nothing, as in my day even the pagans understood. Politicians such as the trifling Pilatus will barter Truth to save their careers – or their skins. Take rather the noble Seneca as your model – or one I have admired in the Beyond: England's own Thomas More: each withstood an arrogant and lustful potentate...

JIM: Yes, well More is somewhat controverted these days – presented rather as a persecutor...

AUSTIN: As I myself, as you note – and I own with some truth, in that I fiercely opposed the Donatists as wreckers of the new-established City of God. Yet we should judge by the standards and the statutes of the times. Great souls will always be pilloried for the ambitions of the petty: hence for the Truth for which the martyrs suffer you substitute Opinion, with none to judge whose opinion is more right than another's: no standard whereby to judge, nor any absolute, whereby to discriminate between *superior* and *inferior*...

PITT: Comparative adjectives of two terminations, adopted into English as nouns: better might be neuter: *superius, inferius*.

DOVE: Thank you, Pitt; I hope we understand what is after all our own language – although sometimes I am, it is true, forced to

doubt it! But if I might put in a word – as an historian merely....
That view, if not begun, was consolidated in the Reformation
when Luther found to his chagrin that every man-jack that could
read – and not a few who could not – would set himself up to
interpret the Scriptures as he pleased, threatening anarchy as each
competed to gloss the Word of God! The bolder formed sects
against which restraints became necessary to their 'enthusiasm'
– that word then denoting being on fire: 'spiritually', that is.
Obstinate Catholics were of course attainted as traitors: hence
cruelties – Bishop Austin is right to this extent – more spectacular
than anything under his edicts: more reminiscent of the Roman
amphitheatre, and I might add just as popular!

JIM: Thank you, Dove. So perhaps you will tell us how from all
that we arrived where we are?

DOVE: Oh – when enough had grown sick of such spectacles
as offered on the Tyburn Tree: particularly handy that for
disemboweling and hanging four men at a time – with the
occasional woman. Or in the case specifically of Catholics, after
the so-called Popish Plot had been revealed to be the malicious
fabrication of Titus Oates: after that, though outlawed they were
increasingly tolerated until Catholic Emancipation – resulting
not least from the part played by Irish soldiers in Wellington's
campaigns against Napoleon.

JIM: Thank you, Dove, again. And so you see, Austin, we arrive
at our present-day toleration and according of each man's – and
each woman's – rights. All under the banner of Freedom.

AUSTIN: That which I find termed Liberalism, from my language's
word for free?

JIM: Pitt! [*kicking a nodding Bones under the table*] Liberalism
– yours, I think!

PITT: Liberalism? Ah from Latin, yes: *liberalis –is –e:* adjective of
two terminations. Free or – ah – liberal: pertaining to a free man –
or of course woman, though perhaps not: that may be why it has
no distinct feminine declension. Connected to – ah- *liber*, a book,
also *libra* a balance, also a pound – that is in weight, but giving
us our pound sterling, being originally a pound *avoirdupois* in
silver (or was it gold...?): hence the ornate 'L' used to denote it.
Also to *liberi* – children of, er, either sex, although the noun itself
is masculine: children I suppose thought of as free, or coming, it
might be, rather too freely – ha-ha! Then *artes liberales* ...

JIM [*hurriedly*]:   Yes, Pitt, thank you for that very comprehensive answer.

DOVE: The Bishop, as I think we all *do* know, had some experience of the untimely coming of a *liber*!

PITT: Not found in the singular. It was perhaps singular for them – *liberi*, I mean – so to come – ha! ha!

JIM [*Coughs*]:   I should clarify that Bishop Redivivus has consented to be interviewed on the understanding there shall be no questions of a purely personal nature...

DOVE: Oh come! This is the BBC!

AUSTIN: You allude, Professor Key-Starr, to my unregenerate days as a Manichee, when – but even now I cannot without pain recall my dearest son Adeodatus and his unhappy mother...

PITT: *A-deo-datus*: God-given...

AUSTIN: Indeed, for as Manichees we would not have, as we saw it, inflicted life upon another. I observe this same Manichean temper pertaining among the so-called whites today (I myself am, your listeners should know, of the swarthier Berber race): a reluctance to reproduce themselves which... But God overruled our selfishness, both giving us a son and taking him to pray for us among His saints.

DOVE: And her – your...

AUSTIN: My concubine – as she could only be; and not being able to make her my lawful wife, I soon determined I would have none.

JIM: Yes, well – that clears that up and now to move on! Where were we? Freedom, I think, and – yes, Austin?

AUSTIN: I would ask about these Rights. Who accords them?

JIM: That's an easy one! The Law, of course!

AUSTIN: And does everyone have every Right under the Law?

JIM: If they can claim them. The lawyers do very well out of it!

AUSTIN: Ah, so these Rights are not so self-evident?

JIM: Well, some more so than others. The American Declaration puts it very well: 'Life, Liberty and the Pursuit of Happiness.'

AUSTIN: Ah, the Pursuit of Happiness! What will make *any* man happy? And Life – *anyone's* life?

JIM: Well, there are disputes about the hopelessly infirm or senile – and of course the unborn, if you count them as lives – and some would say infants below a certain stage...

AUSTIN: They may be killed?

JIM: Might be – depending. Mercifully, if possible, of course.

AUSTIN: So those who survive have these Rights – if they can claim them! And the other one, Liberty: is it perhaps the origin of this admired creed of Liberalism?

JIM: I suppose so. More or less. It all goes back to the Enlightenment, you see, and the French Revolution that brought it about. And of course the American Revolution.

AUSTIN: Just so; I have read of these Revolutions: more especially that most bloodthirsty French one – in its time anathema, as I understand, to you English, yet now it seems... But so one must expect when the living God is expelled from human affairs; it now appears that even your nation's proclaimed Liberalism is born of that Liberty that deified Reason, placing her as an idol even in the shrine of God's Mother, to preside over your then-enemies' cataclysm!

JIM: Well, I suppose so. Seems a bit extreme, that. Better ask Dove here.

DOVE: I would say rather it was the imposition of the will of the strong – in this case, as in other Revolutions, touted as the Will of the People!

[*Silence until Austin resumes*]

AUSTIN: That cannot surprise me. I learned in Oxford how an older understanding of *voluntas* had been lost – even perverted into a supposed faculty, designated the Will, whereby men of strong 'will' might impose on lesser men!

JIM: Or women, of course. Or the ungendered. Pitt?

PITT: Ah yes, *voluntas, voluntatis*, noun feminine and abstract of the third declension: as the bishop says, in earlier Latin may denote rather a disposition or willingness, not normally as strong as our cognate word 'will' – deriving, it appears, its force from its German cognate, in modern German *Die Wille*.

JIM: Thank you, Pitt. Austin?

AUSTIN: Indeed I have taken the will to be rightly understood as the positive expression of love's outflowing. But I return to this creed of Liberalism, which I admit intrigues me. It does not, I must suppose, permit *everything*?

JIM [*relieved*]:   Oh no! No, no: you can't catch us out there, ha! ha! By no means! It is agreed – it is understood that it permits *everything that does not harm another!*

AUSTIN: But surely that were hardly to be assessed! Falsity, to begin with, needs must harm others – and multiply its effects upon a society...

JIM: Hence we limit the restriction to *obvious* harm.

AUSTIN: And thus the ancient serpent works his guile – the better for being unseen – in the *not obvious*!

JIM: The Devil, you mean? [*laughs forcedly*]. Well, of course we don't believe in a devil any more!

AUSTIN: Ah no? Perhaps only in his – what do you call them in your politics? – his 'slogans': such as 'obvious harm'! And yet you have churchmen still, and bishops!

JIM: We do – of course. And now church-women: priests, even bishops!

AUSTIN: That indeed is some novelty, albeit in my day they might, once widowed, be deaconesses. Paula, who studied with Hieronymus, was highly regarded. And pious women like my beloved mother Monnica did much good among the faithful. But do these churchmen – and now women – not believe in the Devil, to whom Scripture attests in Our Lord's own words?

JIM: Very few of them; they regard him – it – as metaphorical.

AUSTIN: I see! And do they accept this slogan, as I call it, of No Obvious Harm?

JIM: In the main they do – apart from some purists, usually of the less instructed class: mainly Evangelicals – especially the black ones – and increasing numbers of Roman Catholics are becoming more pliant...

AUSTIN: In what respect more pliant?

JIM: Oh, you know, in what used to be thought of as morality: practices formerly frowned on in religion – sexual practices in particular, which clearly can harm no-one if not the practitioners. Contraception – pretty well accepted by all; the rising divorce-rate – now restrained by the fact that ever fewer get married in the first place. Abortion, homosexuality – a recent Archbishop of Canterbury has proposed a complete revision of Christian sexual ethics, and even the Pope, we hear...

AUSTIN: You surely are not telling me of practices that do no harm – even obvious harm! Divorce? Abortion?

JIM: Well, the balance of harm and good is controversial and where that is the case it is left to the individual... Besides, we are hardly a majority Christian country any more, nor indeed continent – many have come from beyond Europe bringing with them their creeds – Buddhism, Islam, Sikhism... And we have revivals of older European cults: druidism, witchcraft...

AUSTIN: Witchcraft! Can that be thought to do no obvious harm?

JIM: Oh, it's very light stuff, quite fanciful – appeals to the women, dancing around and calling on the powers of Mother Earth, you know! The Buddhists, of course, believe in reincarnation, which keeps them in order – the prospect of being a spider or a toad next time round: all quite harmless, and peaceful – usually.

AUSTIN: But is it true!

JIM: Well, it can't be, of course – certainly not all of it. But I suppose as true as most of people's notions. After all, what is Truth?

AUSTIN: That question has been posed before. And the answer in the past was clear enough: the Word of God!

JIM: Yes, well, that was then. Since then we have had Science!

AUSTIN: In my day and language, science – *scientia* – meant knowledge: what you can *know*.

[*Beneath the table Summe-Geeze's foot fails to contact a by now nodding Bones*]

JIM: Er – yes, I think we all remember that much Latin from those schooldays of yore: makes me feel quite old, ha! ha! Science of course means knowledge!

AUSTIN: Only now it seems it is confined to matters of physics – of nature as you say: *De Rerum Natura*, as the Epicurean Lucretius put it [*Jim looks hopelessly in the direction of Pitt Bones*]: of how things *work*, as you so strangely express it in your language.

JIM: Well, yes; at least what we can find out. Beyond that is speculation.

AUSTIN: In my day that was *learning how*, rather than understanding.

JIM: But we do understand – more and more – how the Universe, er – *works*.

AUSTIN: The Universe – the sum total! You may continue to find out more and more, probably ad *infinitum*! [*Summe-Geeze looks nervously towards Bones*] Or until, as the Psalmist puts it, the moon fail!

PITT [*belatedly*]:   Aha! The English subjunctive – falling sadly into disuse!

AUSTIN: Yet will you not understand how it came to be, not ever by the power of your 'science', being limited to the Universe itself, to matter...

JIM: Matter has been shown to be non-material, you know!

AUSTIN: Yet still, in all its manifestations, still of nature: *physis* as the Greeks called her – from which your Physics. Still, as I must put it, *created*!

JIM: Yes, well, perhaps that is all we *can* know, but it is enough to keep us going a long time!

AUSTIN: Long or short, the End will come – or before that shall this false 'knowledge', this *scientia* of yours, destroy you, it seems!

JIM: One devoutly hopes not!

AUSTIN: Ah, devoutly! *De voto* : in accordance with your vow! [*Unexpectedly BONES mutters "Correct! Votum, neuter of the second declension: a vow – from which 'votive'!"*] Vow to whom, I wonder?

JIM: Yes, well, these are outmoded speech-forms.

AUSTIN: And your surviving churchmen – and women? Do I understand they have given up Theology?

JIM: Oh no! We have Departments of Theology – or anyway of Religious Studies – in many of our Universities!

AUSTIN: Indeed, I have spoken with some from these Departments: I would call the best among them scholars of the Scriptures, rather than heirs to Ambrosius, Hieronymus or my poor self! Nor even to those I learned came after: Gregorius, Bernard, Thomas – your Oxford's Scotus, Newman...

JIM: I believe there were still some French theologians among the Catholics, around the time of the Council – the Second Vatican Council, that is. Now, as I understand, there is the influence of German philosophy: Hegel, Kant, Nietzsche. They, of course, are children of the Reformation.

AUSTIN: I have heard these names, but not that they were any kind of Christians, these philosophers.

JIM: Hardly – indeed in the case of Nietzsche, decidedly *anti*! Hegel believed in Historicism: the Thesis Antithesis-Synthesis that gave rise to Marx. Some German theologians, as I understand, follow Hegel.

AUSTIN: Then have they no place for Christ in such a Universe?

JIM: Well, not as divine, clearly. As a Jewish Rabbi – hardly perhaps for Nietzsche, and I presume Hegelian churchmen... But these are deep waters for our listeners.

AUSTIN: Indeed, as for myself! I find it hard to understand how Christian theologians can be swayed by these anti-Christian philosophers – as it seems they term themselves, albeit *philosophia* means Love of Wisdom. Plato, as I conceive, would rather term them *Sophistai*!

JIM: No, no! They are highly respected – by those that have read them! Including of course the theologians.

AUSTIN: Indeed, who thence fail to stand on what should be their proper ground, as I have observed in the Oxford debating chamber!

JIM: Well, I don't think they quite know what that ground might be, or if it exists!

DOVE: They rather lack subject-matter since Form Criticism has applied itself to the Scriptures!

AUSTIN: I have heard of this Form Criticism which has come also out of Germany and the Reformation. Giving up the primacy of the Church – as if there could be valid Scriptures without that! From where do they think they come?

DOVE: From the Holy Spirit, wasn't it?

AUSTIN: Assuredly so, since the same Scriptures record the Lord's promise that the disciples – the Church he founded – should be led by the Spirit 'into all Truth'. But the Spirit was sent upon those disciples, upon the infant church, before any of the Gospels were written, before even the Letters of Paul...

JIM: At all events, they would be uneasy – think it bad form, you know, to introduce – that is, for a Theologian to set him – er, or her-self, or let us say themselves – against an Oxford Philosopher!

AUSTIN: In my time, Theologian and Philosopher was the same calling, or rather what you distinguish as 'theology' joined with Philosophy to illumine that Truth already apprehended by the best of the pagans – Plato, Aristotle; even the Stoics in part consonant with Revelation, because all seeking the one Truth!

JIM: Ah, truth again! Truth is nowadays more or less agreed to be Relative!

AUSTIN: To what relative?

JIM: To – well, the times, you know! Or the culture. Or the individual.

AUSTIN: You astonish me! I should have supposed the True and the Relative to be mutually exclusive concepts!

JIM: Yes, well, of course there are those who would still agree with you on that, but...

AUSTIN: Yes?

JIM: But they are less often heard from. Hardly a popular stance with *l'homme moyen-sensuel* – You understand French? Or as we express it, "the man on the Clapham omnibus"!

AUSTIN: Ah *omnibus*! You refer to the wider populace: the sheep that their Lord would pasture?

JIM: That reminds me of something – Milton, isn't it? 'The hungry sheep look up and are not fed!'

AUSTIN: Indeed! But your interesting French phrase, which I a little understand from Latin as *homo medius sensualis*, is it not? And is he – or she [*BONES perks up momentarily to interject: "Correct! Homo, gender common!"*] to be the judge?

JIM: The man on the Clapham omnibus? By no means! Nor the woman neither, though in this case I think we assume gender-masculine. [*AUSTIN looks puzzled.*] But the man – or woman – at the Hampstead dinner-party: it would be hard to prevent them being the judges, since they are on the government committees and the NGOs and the editorial boards of the most approved newspapers and now in the blogosphere – to say nothing of the BBC and other media!

AUSTIN: And who appoints them to such posts of worldly power?

JIM: They appoint each other, of course.

AUSTIN: And can none oppose them?

JIM: Some try, but rarely if ever succeed, being swiftly excluded – or they learn to conform.

AUSTIN: And the remaining churchmen – the bishops, say?

JIM: Oh, they are among the readiest to conform. They look on it as Christian charity.

AUSTIN: Indeed! And can charity consist with falsity? I would suppose they would at least stand out and challenge these supposed orthodoxies and the self-appointed preachers thereof!

JIM: Should they do so – as you know, we have debates, perhaps more politely conducted within the Faculties themselves than in the debating chambers of our Universities: as even on occasion on the BBC – but the Christians always end up with minority support.

AUSTIN: Is it that the majority are – as one would expect – the *sensuales* who fear the curtailing of their lusts? Or is it rather that these would-be champions yet appear insincere in their arguments? Or do they perchance out of self-doubt cede ground unnecessarily to their opponents?

JIM: I grant you it could be all the above! Of course, debating is a matter of knowing how to support either side of an argument…

AUSTIN: That in older times was known as the art of Sophistry – or better of Lying! I myself practised it, alas, before my conversion!

JIM: Really? But then no-one likes to appear behind the times!

AUSTIN: Yet is Truth for *all* times, and the Faith *quod ab omnibus, omni tempore…*

PITT [*unexpectedly*]:   Newman! In his *Apologia*! A quotation – is it from yourself?

AUSTIN: I may well have used it against the aforesaid Donatists. Yet in Newman's day was not the great Apostasy already under weigh?

JIM: Way? Oh, I see, 'weigh', as from weighing an anchor!

AUSTIN: Just so. Had not the ship of your English state been sailing these troubled waters ever since your King Henry cast off her anchor from Christ's chosen Rock, Petros?

JIM: You could say that, I suppose, and we know that's how Catholics see it – Roman Catholics, that is…

DOVE: Really, Jim, you do know, I suppose, there are other Catholics – Maronites, Melkites, some Copts – who plainly see it the same way or they wouldn't be where they are – even have chosen to be, as the Uniates: though I'd be surprised if even the Orthodox didn't see it, since that so plainly is what happened – for good or ill, and I would say for both. It takes special pleading to see it otherwise. After all, Luther himself remarked that Henry wanted to play God!

JIM: Still, a bit fanciful, all that about the ship! We are a seafaring nation – or were: not surprising if we wanted to shake off mainland Europe! [*intones*] 'Britons never, never, never shall be slaves!' [*Austin looks puzzled.*] Just a song that used to be popular – now perhaps only once a year at the Proms.

AUSTIN: Yet to my observation your countrymen – and more especially your women – appear enslaved to an all-pervasive what is called Consumerism – worshipped in a multitude of shrines you designate shops, and Department Stores with glass and lights more dazzling than in the noble cathedrals I have admired...

JIM: Well. Of course Commerce – and the dear old GDP, eh, Dove?

DOVE: Certainly we need to hold our own in the markets of the world – and yet I am somewhat of Austin's view that it becomes what he would call idolatry. Useful, of course, to keep the masses occupied with acquisition – and then the disposal of all the stuff!

AUSTIN: And do all take part in this idolatry?

JIM: Of shopping? I'm afraid we all do – or at least our partners for us.

AUSTIN: Partners?

JIM: Wives if you like. Except not married. And not necessarily women. Husbands too, of course – not necessarily men...

AUSTIN: You mean..?

JIM: I mean 'partner' is a usefully nonjudgmental term. But to reply to your question: There are of course some who cannot afford to do much shopping.

AUSTIN [*as if to himself*]:   'The poor you have always with you.' And – ah – what do they do?

JIM S-S: Mainly sit at home – if they have a home, that is – and watch TV: very good for the Ratings and of course provides an at least vicarious experience, more especially the commercial channels. Or sit in the park – Our parks, you will have noticed, are numerous and well supplied with benches. And of course they must get out regularly to the Job-centre and sign on for Benefits. We have good Social Security in this country, you know. In the last resort – for foreigners or other indigents who fall between the stools – know what I mean? – there are set up Soup Kitchens where they can obtain food.

AUSTIN: I am glad to hear it; and yet, 'Man does not live by bread alone.' What do the Bishops have to say about all this?

JIM: Quite a lot, really. It's what they're mostly on about. Very left-leaning lot on the whole; they find it a subject on which they can make themselves be heard, even by government.

AUSTIN: But do they not preach charity – and self-restraint?

JIM: Up to a point. Not self-restraint much: perhaps giving up chocolate or beer for Lent. And charity has rather a bad name, you know: it's mainly left to NGOs and organizations like

Oxfam – which of course churches urge us to support, financially and in other ways.

AUSTIN: These churches – how many are there?

JIM: Don't ask me to count! Of course, most of them are very minority now, like the Methodists; the Baptists perhaps stronger, especially among black folk; the Presbyterians – mainly in Scotland: Her Majesty the Queen becomes a Presbyterian when she crosses the Border; the Congregationalists – almost died out. Most of us say we are CofE – Church of England, that is – regardless...

AUSTIN: Ah, the Erastians – as in time the Caesaro-papists of my day would be called – and yes, your Queen is their Head, is she not?

JIM: No, no. Supreme Governor is her title.

AUSTIN: I see. And their Bishops sit in the Parliament?

JIM: Some, yes. Not yet the Bishopesses, though that will come, I trust.

AUSTIN: You are yourself of the CofE, as you name your national church?

JIM: Yes, rather; I mean not being anything else, we pretty well all are. And you realize it's not only in England. There's the Anglican Communion. In the USA they're called Episcopalians.

AUSTIN: Ah yes, I have been apprised of a certain controversy there which in deference to St Paul we should leave unnamed.

JIM: Yes, quite right. We all know what you mean but this is not the place to pursue it. No doubt an accommodation will be found; that is the beauty of being an Anglican: I mean pretty well anything goes short of murder – these days at least. We've come a long, long way.

AUSTIN: And the remaining Catholics? Their bishops, as I understand, do not sit in the Parliament.

JIM: Not thus far. An older Pope forbade that. Of course many of the CofE clergy claim to *be* Catholic and the CofE the Catholic Church in England.

AUSTIN: Despite the schism and the break with Rome?

DOVE: Speaking as an outsider to all this – and adapting the saying of the inimitable Mandy Rice-Davies of blessed memory: 'Well, they would, wouldn't they!' Henry the Eighth took the same view of his position after Clement disowned him: Catholic without the Pope. His successors – perhaps *pace* some Laudians – took a more robust view, decrying popes and all their work as 'the anti-Christ of Rome'. Down to Newman who did his best to make the case, and we know how *he* ended up!

AUSTIN: Ah yes, a Cardinal and now Blessed – perhaps to be raised to the altars: this I learned in Oxford and read some of his remarkable writings. But in all this, as I noticed before, I perceive you English are become at best Pelagians – indeed I seem to recall the heretic Pelagius himself was from these islands – hence perhaps his name.

PITT [*puts in hurriedly*]: *pelagius*: adjective masculine of first and second declension, meaning 'of the sea'.

AUSTIN: But the Catholics – the Roman Catholics if you will.

JIM: Oh, they're not so very different from the rest these days. Most quite liberal, despite some recent popes. Not all, of course; some still cling to older beliefs and would even if the pope told them they didn't need to anymore!

AUSTIN: Ah, you mean a remnant... We believe, based on Scripture, it is a remnant that will be saved!

JIM: Others say the same – the Jehovah Witnesses, for example. But no-one much believes anyone is not 'saved', as you put it. Not in the twenty-first century!

AUSTIN: Ah – that might help explain the rather, shall we say colourless society you describe and I encounter...

DOVE: You've said it! Utterly boring – and humourless! The English used to be famous for their humour: now all clamped down on by the Hampstead people and the Oxford people and their emulators up and down the land with their 'political correctitudes' – and don't try to poke fun or you'll end up in court! I know them – meet them among my colleagues at Chattering! If you ask me, a lot of bloody Philistines, as I'm sure the rather refreshing Bishop must find them, only is too polite to say so! What happened to art, or poetry – and I don't mean what that crowd chooses to puff in their incestuous little circles...

JIM: Er – Thank you, Professor Key-Starr; we always appreciate your own brand of refreshing frankness! Our thanks too to Professor Bones, and of course Bishop Austin whom we are so privileged to have as our guest. Sadly we have come to the end of our time, though I am sure we could continue this – er – stimulating discussion. Thank you all. This is James Summe-Geeze preparing to hand our listeners over to our next programme: The Moral Maze...

AUSTIN [*fading out*]: O Beauty, forever ancient and ever new...

FURTHER READING

For my discussion of the influence of Augustine over the centuries, see J.M. Rist, *Augustine Deformed* (Cambridge University Press 2014).

I list works on Augustine's ideas and other books in English – plus two in Italian relevantly related and one in French – which I have found especially useful in composing the present text, as follows:

Arquillière, H.-X., *L'Augustinisme politique* (second revised edition). Paris, Vrin 1933.

Brown, P., *Augustine of Hippo* (revised edition). London, Faber and Faber 2000.

Bruno, M.J.S., *Political Augustinianism: Modern Interpretations of Augustine's Political Thought*. Minneapolis, MN, Fortress Press 2014.

Burnell, P., *The Augustinian Person*. Washington, DC, Catholic University of America Press 2005.

Canning, R., *The Unity of Love of God and Neighbour in Saint Augustine*. Leuven 1993.

Cory, T.S., 'Diachronically Unified Consciousness in Augustine and Aquinas', *Vivarium* 50 (2012) 354–381.

Couenhoven, J., *Stricken by Sin, Cured by Christ: Agency, Necessity and Culpability in Augustinian Theology*. Oxford University Press 2013.

Dodaro, R., *Christ and the Just Society in the Thought of Augustine*. Cambridge University Press 2004.

Fredriksen, P., *Augustine and the Jews: A Christian Defense of Jews and Judaism*. New York, Doubleday 2008.

Hollingworth, M., *The Pilgrim City: St Augustine of Hippo and His Innovation in Political Thought*. London, T&T Clark 2010.

Karfikova, L., *Grace and the Will according to Augustine*. Leiden, Brill 2012.

Malo, A., *Io e gli Altri: dall'identità alla relazione*. Rome, EDUSC 2010.

Malo, A., *Essere Persona: Un'antropologia dell'identità*. Rome, Armando Editore 2013.

Matthews, G.B., *Thought's Ego in Augustine and Descartes*. Ithaca, Cornell University Press 1992.

Matthews, G.B. (ed.), *The Augustinian Tradition*. Berkeley/Los Angeles /London, University of California Press 1999.

Rist, J.M., *Augustine: Ancient Thought Baptised*. Cambridge University Press 1994.

Sokolowski, R., *Phenomenology of the Human Person*. Cambridge University Press 2009.

Stump, E., and N. Kretzmann, *The Cambridge Companion to Augustine* (first edition). Cambridge University Press 2001.

Talmon, J.L., *The Origins of Totalitarian Democracy*. London, Secker and Warburg 1952.

Wetzel, J. (ed.), *Augustine's City of God: A Critical Guide*. Cambridge University Press 2012.

Wynn, P., *Augustine on War and Military Service*. Minneapolis, MN, Fortress Press 2013.

And for works in English of contemporary friends and foes of Augustine glanced at particularly in the present book:

Darwall, S.L., *The British Moralists and the 'Internal Ought': 1640–1740*. Cambridge University Press 1995.

Dworkin, R., *Taking Rights Seriously*. London, Duckworth 1977.

Frankfurt, H., *The Importance of What We Care About*. Cambridge University Press 1988.

Fromm, E., *The Art of Loving*. London, Harper and Rowe 1956.

Gregory, B., *The Unintended Reformation*. Cambridge, MA, Harvard University Press 2012.

Hart, H.L.A., *The Concept of Law*. Oxford University Press 1961.

Hunt, L., *Inventing Human Rights*. New York/London, Norton 2007.

Kripke, S., *Naming and Necessity*. Cambridge, MA, Harvard University Press 1980.

MacIntyre, A., *After Virtue*. South Bend, Notre Dame University Press 1971.

Manent, P., *An Intellectual History of Liberalism*. Princeton University Press 1994.

Nagel, T., *The View from Nowhere*. New York, Oxford University Press 1986.

Oderberg, D.S., and T.J.D. Chappell, *Human Values, New Essays in Ethics and Natural Law*. London/New York, Palgrave MacMillan 2004.

Parfit, D., *Reasons and Persons*. Oxford University Press 1986.

Rawls, J., *A Theory of Justice*. Cambridge, MA, Harvard University Press 1971.

Rawls, J., *Political Liberalism*. New York, Columbia University Press 1993.

Schneewind, J.B., *The Invention of Autonomy*. Cambridge University Press 1997.

Sidgwick, H., *Methods of Ethics* (seventh edition). London, MacMillan 1907.

Taylor, C., *Sources of the Self*. Cambridge, MA, Harvard University Press 1989.

Waldron, J. (ed.), *Theories of Rights*. Oxford University Press 1984.

INDEX